Praise for T

The next sentence is cliché. ~~...book is the book I have wanted on~~ on leadership. It may be cliché, but it's true. Ron Edmondson is one of the best to bless us with a book on leadership myths. He absolutely nails it. Read this book to become a better leader. Read this book to become a better person.

THOM S. RAINER
PRESIDENT AND CEO
LIFEWAY CHRISTIAN RESOURCES

Everyone thinks they know how to lead until they suddenly find themselves in an actual leadership role. Then they quickly discover that much of what they "know" isn't actually so. If you are a leader, this book will save you a lot of heartache. Ron Edmondson is an experienced leader, who has already paid a lot of the "dumb taxes" for you. I encourage you to carefully read it, apply it, and save yourself a ton of grief.

LARRY OSBORNE
PASTOR AND AUTHOR
NORTH COAST CHURCH

I found *The Mythical Leader* freeing, affirming, and refreshing. You will feel better about yourself as a leader and understand other leaders better. Myths about leadership that have held you and others back will be powerless as you lead with greater confidence than ever before. Thanks, Ron, for your transparency that make this a powerful resource.

SAM CHAND, LEADERSHIP CONSULTANT
AUTHOR OF *BIGGER, FASTER LEADERSHIP* AND *LEADERSHIP PAIN*

Like many, I've been both challenged and encouraged by Ron's writing through the years. What gives his writing power is that he's sharing from the success he's had in both church planting and church revitalization. This book is no different. The principles he shares in *The Mythical Leader* will shape your leadership and help you grow your influence . . . the sign of a real leader.

TONY MORGAN

FOUNDER AND LEAD STRATEGIST OF THE UNSTUCK GROUP

AUTHOR OF *THE UNSTUCK CHURCH*

With so many books out there on leadership, it is hard to know which ones really matter. For me, I want to read books by people who are actually leading well. Ron Edmondson has devoted himself to effective leadership in the local church and has practiced it so well himself. He is a pastor and leader respected by many. What a gift that he would take time to write a book to dispel myths that limit the leadership potential of so many people. If you are looking to take your leadership to the next level, this is the book for you!

JIM SHEPPARD

CEO AND PRINCIPAL, GENERIS

CO-AUTHOR, *CONTAGIOUS GENEROSITY*

I've been on a lifelong quest to figure out leadership. I wish I had seen this book when I began! Ron has defused many of the myths I wasted time on early in my career. Read this book, and you'll save time and hassle in your own journey as a leader.

WILLIAM VANDERBLOEMEN

PRESIDENT AND FOUNDER

VANDERBLOEMEN SEARCH GROUP

The Mythical Leader encourages, challenges, and inspires you to be a better leader. Ron Edmondson mentors you with every page he's written. I found his transparent storytelling and practical wisdom refreshing. What I valued most is that he effectively dispels all the myths that prevent leaders from humbly leading with God-honoring excellence.

TAMI HEIM
PRESIDENT AND CEO
CHRISTIAN LEADERSHIP ALLIANCE

Ron Edmondson's *The Mythical Leader* is a deceptively simple read, but don't mistake simplicity for easy. As you uncover the truth behind each of the seven leadership myths, you will find yourself becoming a more impactful leader.

SKIP PRICHARD, CEO
AUTHOR OF *THE BOOK OF MISTAKES*
LEADERSHIP INSIGHTS BLOGGER AT WWW.SKIPPRICHARD.COM

Ron pulls from his experiences as a business leader, community leader, and church leader to assemble a great book to debunk the seven myths of leadership. It is a must-read if you are new to leadership, have a desire to be a better leader, or just want to have a greater impact with those around you.

STU RAMSEY, PRESIDENT/CEO
PEN AIR FEDERAL CREDIT UNION

The Mythical Leader is outstanding! Ron Edmondson is an incredible leader who has been a lifelong learner in the area of leadership. I'm so glad he's written this book to share principles I've personally witnessed him apply and achieve excellent and long lasting results. Put this book in an easy-to-reach area because you will be referencing it many times as you face leadership myths in your life.

JOSEPH SANGL
PRESIDENT AND CEO
INJOY STEWARDSHIP SOLUTIONS

Ron has written an earthy book about leadership, one with the unmistakable grittiness of lived experience. Long on concrete examples and short on abstract leadership theory, the book is more like a how-to manual than a philosophy text. It offers an inside glimpse into the life and calling of a gifted leader.

Tim Hall
President
Mercy College, New York

Ron Edmondson has been a friend and a leader I have admired for many years. He has waded the difficult waters of leadership with a steady perseverance and commitment that feels all too rare in today's culture. His new book, *The Mythical Leader*, is an absolute essential for every young leader who wants to lead well for the long haul. Both practical and personal, this book will equip you with valuable leadership wisdom from a proven and trustworthy leader.

Jenni Catron
Founder of The 4Sight Group and
Author of *The 4 Dimensions of Extraordinary Leadership*

Ron Edmondson helps every leader overcome their biggest obstacle to success, bad thinking. In *The Mythical Leader*, Ron helps leaders tackle the myths that keep them from the success and fulfillment they desire.

David Chrzan
Chief of Staff
Saddleback Church

The Mythical Leader

The Mythical Leader

Seven Myths of Leadership

RON EDMONDSON

THOMAS NELSON
Since 1798

Published in Nashville, Tennessee, by Thomas Nelson. Thomas Nelson is a registered trademark of HarperCollins Christian Publishing, Inc.

Thomas Nelson titles may be purchased in bulk for educational, business, fund-raising, or sales promotional use. For information, please e-mail SpecialMarkets@ ThomasNelson.com.

ISBN 978-0-7180-8919-1 (softcover)
ISBN 978-0-7180-8924-5 (e-book)

Library of Congress Cataloging-in-Publication Data

Names: Edmondson, Ron, author.
Title: The mythical leader : the seven myths of leadership / Ron Edmondson.
Description: Nashville : Thomas Nelson, 2017. | Includes bibliographical references.
Identifiers: LCCN 2016044065 | ISBN 9780718089191
Subjects: LCSH: Christian leadership. | Leadership. | Leadership—Religious aspects—Christianity.
Classification: LCC BV652.1 .E385 2017 | DDC 253—dc23 LC record available at https://lccn.loc.gov/2016044065

Printed in the United States of America
17 18 19 20 21 RRD 10 9 8 7 6 5 4 3 2 1

For my über-loyal wife, Cheryl. You wrote the book on what a wife should be. (Or at least you should.) Thanks for loving me even when I'm not very lovable.

ABOUT Leadership✻Network

LEADERSHIP NETWORK FOSTERS INNOVATION MOVEMENTS that activate the church to greater impact. We help shape the conversations and practices of pacesetter churches in North America and around the world. The Leadership Network mindset identifies church leaders with forward-thinking ideas—and helps them to catalyze those ideas, resulting in movements that shape the church.

Together with HarperCollins Christian Publishing, the biggest name in Christian books, the NEXT imprint of Leadership Network moves ideas to implementation for leaders to take their ideas to form, substance, and reality. Placed in the hands of other church leaders, that reality begins spreading from one leader to the next . . . and to the next . . . and to the next, where that idea begins to flourish into a full-grown movement that creates a real, tangible impact in the world around it.

NEXT: A LEADERSHIP NETWORK RESOURCE COMMITTED TO HELPING YOU GROW YOUR NEXT IDEA.

LEADNET.ORG/NEXT

 **CONTENTS**

 **ACKNOWLEDGMENTS**

TO JESUS CHRIST, MY SAVIOR AND THE GREATEST EXAMPLE of leadership to me. Thanks for trusting this business-minded person into leadership in your church.

To my wife: you got the dedication, but you deserve thanks for allowing me the time away and time of head fog to write this book. You are my greatest supporter.

To my boys, Jeremy and Nate: you two are my most trusted advisors. Thanks for taking time to read parts of this ahead of time and offer suggestions that made the book better. (I hope you'll read the rest.)

To the readers of my blog and my followers on social media: you inspire me to keep writing. You're a huge part of this!

To the staff at Immanuel: there were sacrifices on your part. And one of them was the days of distraction I faced during the heaviest writing days. Thanks for being a great team.

To Immanuel Baptist Church: thanks for being a kingdom-minded church and seeing my role in kingdom growth as bigger than inside our building.

To the people with Leadership Network: you've been a great influence on my ministry and leadership.

To the team at Thomas Nelson: you made this process so easy! Thank you.

To Mark Sweeney: we kept trying to find the right book. You suggested this one first. Thank you.

To Don Gates: you're a great agent. Thank you!

 **INTRODUCTION**

I WILL NEVER FORGET THE FRANTIC CALL I RECEIVED FROM Mark, a sharp young pastor. He had gone to another church just six months earlier, and he was excited about some of the things he had learned while serving in the larger church. He had great energy, vision, and enthusiasm. Now, six months later, he was wondering if it was time to look elsewhere. Nothing the search team had told him was true. People weren't ready for change. They resisted everything he tried to do. Shortly after his arrival, he went from receiving numerous Sunday lunch invitations to fewer invitations and more anonymous e-mails written in all caps.

This young, big-hearted pastor said to me as we neared the end of our conversation, "I didn't know it was going to be this hard to lead here." He had apparently entered the position with a lot of preconceived myths about leadership.

I wish he were the only one who came to mind whenever I tell his story.

John Maxwell, one of our favorite leadership experts, said leadership is influence.[1] A friend of mine repeatedly says, "Everything rises and falls on leadership." I love simple definitions and explanations. Simple works. Many times, less is more, and simple is effective.

While I believe those words may simplify what leadership is, experience has taught me the actual practice of leading is much more complicated. When I have observed real leadership—the kind of leadership that revitalizes a plateaued church, begins a movement to address human trafficking, or reverses a declining business—it is often not easy to define in a few simple words. In fact, people who aren't actually in leadership—those who have never led anything—exhibit a lot of myths when it comes to what leadership means and certainly how it's practiced.

I regularly encounter people in positions of leadership—that is, they hold a title—and they certainly influence people. But when you observe their organizations, you often note their lack of success and attribute it to the absence of good leadership. This problem has never been more prevalent in the church than now, when more than 80 percent of churches are considered plateaued or dying.

I believe much of this is due to a misunderstanding of what leadership is and what it isn't. In my work with hundreds of pastors and churches, the single most common need I find—and most pastors and many congregants recognize this—is the need for more effective leadership in the local church. Seminaries may prepare pastors to preach, just as colleges may prepare teachers to teach, but who prepares people to lead in the church?

In my long career in business and government leadership, and now after serving in church planting and church revitalization, I've found the problems churches face are generally the same. We need better leadership.

I need to warn you about something, however. Even though I have said leadership is not an easy subject to apply, this is a simple book, mostly because I'm a simple person. I like to take complicated subjects and simplify them. Honestly, when I think about some of these principles, they appear to be common sense to me now, although I realize they weren't always. Still, I don't expect a lot of *wow* moments in this book. I'm not going to use a bunch of definitions or textbook-worthy research on leadership. You might find a few Tweet-worthy points, but I simply want to expose some of the common misunderstandings of leadership, share stories from my own experience, and I hope, even if only for a few people, help develop healthier patterns to improve individual leadership skills.

As I write this, I wish I could illustrate my heart to you in this matter. I love leaders. I love investing in leaders. Every time I talk with leaders—such as the pastor I mentioned above—my heart goes out to them. I've been there. I have the T-shirt, but I refuse to wear it because it hurts too much. I have some huge scars from my thirty-plus years in leadership positions. But reflecting on where I am today and the way God has allowed us to see the fruit of our leadership, especially in the last decade of ministry, as the old saying goes, I wish I had known then some of the things I know now. This is why I have blogged for so many years and ultimately why I'm writing this book now.

My hope for this book is that it will encourage, challenge, and inspire you to be a better leader. In the church, in the marketplace, and in our communities, we need better leaders. I believe this is true in our current society more than ever before. Let's get started!

 **MYTH 1**

A Position Will Make Me a Leader

MY FIRST PAID LEADERSHIP ROLE CAME BY DEFAULT. I WAS a full-time college student working in the men's department of a large retail department store. I had been at the store less than two years when my boss suddenly quit. Turnover is high in the retail world, but it seemed even more than normal in this department. Since I was the most tenured person on staff, they made me the new manager.

Looking back, it was probably one of the weaker moments of my leadership journey. I was not at all prepared and made a lot of mistakes.

But it was a huge blessing in my life. I was paying my way through school. The new position gave me some extra money. I moved into a better off-campus apartment, bought nicer clothes, and had better dates.

More so, even though I did not always know what I was doing, it began my professional leadership career. I had previous leadership experience in high school, serving as student body president. But this time I was being paid to lead a group of people.

At twenty years of age, I had basically arrived in the field of leadership.

Are you impressed yet?

If you are not especially impressed, you are in good company with the people I had been challenged to lead.

The store was situated close to a university, so it attracted college students as employees. I remember the first time we had a big sale after I took over the department. Midnight madness sales were popular at that time. We would close for a couple of hours in the late afternoon, cover all our doors with butcher wrap paper to add suspense, then reopen in the evening with significantly marked-down items throughout the store. People would stand in line for hours prior to the sale and scramble to find the bargains as soon as we opened the doors. This type of sale is not as common anymore as people have come to expect bargains daily, either in the store or online. Although it was not quite midnight, it truly was madness. (We later changed these sales to "moonlight madness.")

The men's department was especially busy during these sales. Men, I learned, are often cheap about buying their own clothes, so they are motivated by the perception of dramatically reduced prices. Plus, they seemed to love the idea of chasing a deal.

I scheduled additional staffing for the evening of this first sales event, relying on the advice of others for how many people I should schedule. You can only imagine my disappointment and embarrassment when the doors opened and my grossly understaffed department was flooded with customers. Two employees, both college students, failed to show up to work that night. It was before the days of cell phones, e-mail, or Facebook, and they did not call. I tried calling them but got no response. I was mortified—and angry.

The next day I ran into one of my no-shows on campus. I asked him where he was the night before and why he never called. He told me he had a test and realized he needed to study. He said he meant to call but got distracted. It was not his regularly scheduled day to work, so he assumed he would not be missed.

I stood there wondering how he could justify what he was saying to me. In this moment I realized he did not see me as his boss but rather as another carefree college student. I was his friend, his colleague, his equal. He seemed to think I would understand—he had a test—and could not grasp my frustration. And that made me even more frustrated.

I started working when I was twelve years old. My first job was at a grocery store. I would ride my bike to the store, where I made a dollar an hour, usually working twenty-five to thirty hours a week. We would fill in our time on the back of a bank counter check (ask someone older what those were) and hand it to the cashier to be paid in cash from the register. I was probably naive when it came to working, but I thought my bosses were my bosses. I was to obey them, show them respect, work hard, and try to impress them by giving them more than they asked of me. I know. Silly me, right?

I learned through my moonlight madness experience that

a title does not make you a leader. Some people who have been in positions for years actually still believe having a title makes them a leader. They assume people will look up to them, do what they request, and show them a higher level of respect just because of their job title. It is what I thought, but I learned the hard way it simply is not true.

You can take any title you want—president, manager, boss—and demand to be addressed in a particular way—Mr. Boss, sir, Mr. Boss Sir—but your title alone will not change how people view you.

This is especially true if those you are trying to lead have known you prior to your new title. My fellow college students knew me first as a student. Thus, my leadership position did not translate easily for them.

Frankly—and this is a slightly different subject, but I may as well let you know—I am not a big fan of titles. When we hire someone, we let them create their own title. After we establish a vision for the position, we even let them write their job descriptions. I have learned the title says far less about the person than the person's actions. Your title does not matter. What matters is how you carry out the work you are responsible for doing.

Since my days in retail, however, I have observed this false perception is not limited to inexperienced leaders like I was at the time. I have known people with huge positions whom no one truly follows. They think they are growing in their leadership over time, but really their paychecks are simply getting bigger, and sometimes they even get a bigger or more appealing job title. They may give out orders and command obedience with positional influence, but no one is willingly following their lead. They may be a boss, but I would not call them a leader. People only appear to be following because they need a job.

I wish I were only writing about the business world. I spent most of my career there, and I still feel confident speaking from this perspective. But I am writing about churches too. I am writing about pastors, deacons, elder chairs, and the chairs of the finance, personnel, or pulpit flower committees. It does not matter the church governance or the size of the church; there will be people who believe they have power or authority—that they are leaders—because of their positions.

I was at my first church for a predetermined length of time in a transitional pastor role. Cheryl and I quickly became great friends with the deacon chairman and his family. We had to travel a good distance to the church, so we would find somewhere to crash after the Sunday morning service until the Sunday night service. (Those were long days of ministry.) Often we would find ourselves at this deacon's house. We loved them. Still do.

A few months before our time ended, the deacon chairman and I got into a discussion about a doctrinal issue. It quickly turned pretty intense. Unfortunately, it was in a larger group setting. He asked me a question, I responded, and it went downhill from there. After this one discussion, our relationship was never the same.

I am not sure he had more than a few words to say to me the rest of my time at that church. We were never again invited to their house. We left the church as planned, said good-bye to everyone, including his family, but he never acknowledged our time there. He even summoned me to a called deacons' meeting to offer a formal complaint about a practical issue, of which he had been fully aware and supportive prior to our doctrinal discussion. Thankfully, I had the support of the other deacons, or I would have surely been asked to leave earlier than planned.

What was the reason for the change in our relationship? It was not really a doctrinal issue. There were probably lots of those before this altercation. It was not because of my preaching or my leadership style. He had plenty of experience with those and was always a great encourager to me. It really was not even the words we exchanged.

The reason for the break in our fellowship is that I crossed a sacred line with the one holding the title of deacon chair in the church. I questioned his authority, his power, his position. In this church, no one questioned this position. The one elected to this important role carried the power with the title and, therefore, should have garnered my full support and submission on the issue—whatever the issue might be.

As a new pastor, I learned so many things at this church about leadership and shepherding. I even learned from this deacon chair. As I said, I love him today—we dearly love his family—and I wish things had gone differently. I wish I had initially responded to him differently. Although it may not have made a difference, I wish I'd had the opportunity to see. I certainly learned firsthand, however, that people often assume the power of a title is granted with a position rather than earned by relationship.

As I talk with church leaders every week, it is apparent we have some people attempting positional leadership in our churches. They are strong in title but weak in motivating and managing staff and volunteers. They may chair a committee—perhaps several—but they are not really accomplishing all they could for the kingdom of God. Even if people appear to be doing what they say, they are not really leading people.

KING SAUL VERSUS KING DAVID

We see this myth of positional leaders throughout the Scriptures. Compare, for example, the leadership of King Saul to the leadership of King David.

Saul appeared to let his position get the best of him. He had been given the privilege of being king, but he took things into his own hands, relying on his own wisdom rather than the wisdom of God. Jealousy over David's popularity practically killed Saul and would have several times had it not been for David's character preventing his taking advantage of Saul's vulnerability. Concern over what others thought of him dominated Saul's kingship. Jonathan, his own son, had a hard time defending Saul's honor before David. Though he had everything a king could want—looks, qualities, and pedigree—he ended horribly. "The LORD regretted that He had made Saul king over Israel" (1 Sam. 15:35).

Contrast Saul to David. One of the things I love about David is he did not need a position to lead the people. We are told in Scripture that David was a man after God's own heart (1 Sam. 13:14; Acts 13:22). I believe it is an important point in understanding how David led.

One of my favorite leadership stories is one of David before he assumed the position of king. The story occurs when David was hiding from Saul.

> Then they told David, saying, "Look, the Philistines are fighting against Keilah, and they are robbing the threshing floors."
>
> Therefore David inquired of the LORD, saying, "Shall I go and attack these Philistines?"
>
> And the LORD said to David, "Go and attack the Philistines, and save Keilah." (1 Sam. 23:1–2)

What does a person after God's own heart do when they see a need they can address but which may be overwhelming? Just as David was sensitive to the plight of his people at the hands of a giant named Goliath, even in hiding, David wanted to protect God's people. Consider his first response.

> But David's men said to him, "Look, we are afraid here in Judah. How much more then if we go to Keilah against the armies of the Philistines?" (1 Sam. 23:3)

David had the humility to go to God for wisdom. Keep in mind David was not yet serving as king. He did not have a king's army. In fact, do you remember who David had as his army? "Everyone who was in distress, everyone who was in debt, and everyone who was discontented gathered to him. So he became captain over them. And there were about four hundred men with him" (1 Sam. 22:2). David had a bunch of misfits surrounding him. They were probably street fighters, but they were likely no match for the trained, battle-ready, heavily armored armies he would fight.

But here is why I love this story. Do you notice what David did? Apparently he consulted with his forces. After he spoke with God, he went to his troops. He may have even asked their opinion, because he certainly appears to have allowed it. As much as obedience is critical to being a good soldier, we certainly know how they felt. And so did David. David's men had continually been loyal to him. He could have used his position as their leader and demanded they go. After all, he had already heard from the Lord.

But David was not a positional leader. He did not need a title for his style of leadership. David was a relational leader. He allowed people to speak into his life, even those he was trying to lead. He was respectful of those trying to follow him.

But go through the rest of the story with me. How did David respond once he knew how his team felt about the potential mission?

Once again David inquired of the Lord, and the Lord answered him:

> "Go down to Keilah. For I will deliver the Philistines into your hand." And David and his men went to Keilah and fought with the Philistines, struck them with a mighty blow, and took away their livestock. So David saved the inhabitants of Keilah. (1 Sam. 23:4–5)

We can learn a lot about life and leadership from David in this story. Instead of demanding loyalty, David went back to the

Lord and inquired again. It appears his men did not question him further. David was not a people-pleaser or a people-controller. He was a leader. He was decisive. He was strong, but he was willing to allow his people to be a part of his leadership. He did not try to protect his position. He recognized that people need to be a part of decisions affecting them and the best decisions are made through collaboration. As David built relationships, he found people who willingly followed him.

THE PROBLEM

The problem when people assume others are following a position or a title is they make decisions that negatively impact others, mostly without even knowing it. The "boss has ruled" mentality has injured many people over the years, including people in the church. Rather than building a consensus of opinion, the person with the highest rank makes the call. They pass rules down through the organizational chart as mandates rather than collaborate with their people to make the best decisions for everyone. And the results are usually damaging to the team and others.

Knowing this to be true, when I arrived at a historic, traditional church that needed revitalization, as much as I knew we needed to make some changes, I did not make any major moves in the first year. And when we made what I was told would be the biggest change of all—switching our service times—we took a year to do it. We started the process by soliciting the input of two dozen people who represented every age group in the church. Unlike David, I did not have a clear mandate from God to change the services, so I made it clear we would not move forward without a consensus and buy-in from the people. I knew it would be important to the success of the new time.

A PERSONAL EXAMPLE

Here's an example of how positional leadership plays out in a normal work situation. It may seem silly, but I learned a lot from it. I learned from many of my mistakes in my early days of leadership, but I also learned some things by watching others attempt to lead.

One of my roles in my first retail leadership position was to order the basic items for my department, making sure we always stocked the regular sellers. One of those items was a collar extender. (I do not know if those are used anymore, and I never used one, but basically it was a metal button with a hook that attached to the collar button to accommodate a larger neck than the shirt was made for. A man could still wear a shirt that technically no longer fit him. You know you wanted to know this.) Anyway, we normally kept a couple of boxes in stock. Each box contained a dozen extenders. When we sold out a box, I would order another box. They were not fast sellers, so it did not happen often.

One day we were down to our last box, so I placed an order. But instead of ordering one box of twelve, I incorrectly ordered twelve boxes, which was pretty much enough extenders for a few decades—or maybe more.

I had made a mistake. I did not realize my mistake until the order arrived and the receiving room opened the case of extenders. A senior manager happened to be in there when the mistake was discovered. Lucky me!

How did management—those people with bigger titles than mine—handle the mistake? Well, it was not by using good leadership principles, as I have come to learn.

The morning after the arrival of the case of extenders, a memo was sent to all area managers and every department: "From now on, all orders will need to be signed by a supervisor prior to completion."

Now, maybe there is nothing wrong with having someone sign off on every order. Perhaps it would be a good cross-check for accountability. But I was instantly humiliated, since I knew the memo was a direct response to my mistake. No one had said anything to me. I had not been reprimanded. My mistake was never mentioned directly to me, although I heard the normal scuttlebutt in the break room enough to confirm the storewide memo was prompted by my mistake. The problem was, because of my error, we now had a new policy that affected everyone. And the new mandate slowed things down, because people now had to wait for approval before they could even order basic stock items. The new policy was not accepted well by the other department managers, and it proved to be more of an inconvenience than it was worth. It was not long before no one followed the new policy at all. But for the short term, I was embarrassed in front of my colleagues and coworkers.

Maybe the story does not seem unreasonable to you. You might be wondering how I think it should have been handled. I believe it should have been handled with relational leadership. I should have been called aside and made aware of my mistake (to let me know they knew). I should have been allowed to learn from the experience. If I continued to make the same error, then further action could have been taken. Thankfully, I never made this mistake again.

I should add that these same managers who taught me this lesson also taught me many more positive lessons in leadership and management. I am forever grateful for their investment in me as a young leader. I am drawing from this one incident because it was such a valuable learning experience for me, but I do not mean to devalue their total investment in me in those early years of leading. But these types of situations, in my opinion, seem to happen more when we lead by title than by relational authority. With relational leadership there will almost always be person-to-person conversation.

You might ask what the collar-extender episode taught me.

The short answer is that it helped shape some of my leadership skills. From a big-picture perspective, I learned that weak management never produces the desired result and is never good leadership. Some people with titles simply pass an edict rather than really handle the problem. The following are seven practical things I learned about leadership from this particular experience.

1. *Never send an e-mail (today's memo) to correct an action.*

Regardless of your position, be relational. Address the person. David did not send an e-mail to his men: "Hey guys, this is what God said to me. Let me know what you think. Please reply all." No, he talked directly to the people trying to follow him.

You cannot read a facial expression by e-mail. You have to do the hard work of confronting the real problem, even if it involves people—and, yes, leadership decisions are always more difficult whenever people are involved.

This memo incident made me feel like an instigator of bad will in the company. Although most people did not originally know who the culprit was, word travels fast among coworkers. It was quickly discovered that I was the guilty party. The workers were so used to this form of weak leadership, they did not blame their leaders. Instead, they blamed me for their additional work responsibilities.

2. *Never overreact to a minor issue.*

This was not a major expense to the company. Collar extenders at the time retailed for $1.25 each. It was a $165.00 mistake for a department with several hundred thousand dollars in sales per year. Honestly, had they addressed the memo to me directly, I would have volunteered to buy the excess collar extenders rather than see a needless policy implemented. It ended up costing more in opportunity costs as needless work was placed on others by the addition of another managerial layer to the ordering process. And there is no way to count the negative cost of goodwill lost among the employees.

As leaders, when it comes to correcting people, we need to concentrate on the major issues. We should set good policies and procedures in place, because we need good systems. But we should not stress so much over the minor issues that, in the grand scheme of things, really will not matter much. This only stresses out people and disrupts morale and efficiency.

3. *Never make a new policy in response to a single error.*

Just as you make up a title and assume it will guide the job description, the same can be true of creating a policy. Again, every organization needs good systems and processes, but leadership is about people first and foremost.

I see churches make this error all the time when an issue involves people. Rather than solve the problem, they change everything for everyone. Either in an effort to avoid conflict or under the disguise of grace, we fail to address the real problem if people are involved.

In our established church, before we revised (and greatly shortened) our policies and procedures—which are voted on by the church—we had a policy on folded chairs. It told you what to do when someone borrows chairs and how to handle their return. The church voted on this policy. (True story.) And you can guess how it got there. Someone had borrowed chairs and did not bring them back. Positional leadership calls for a new rule regarding the borrowing of chairs. Relational leadership approaches the person who did not return the chairs and asks, "Hey, you know those chairs that belong to the church that you have in your garage? Would you bring them back?"

The first week I arrived at the church, my assistant handed me a form to fill out and get back to her. I asked her what it was, and she said, "It's your time sheet so you can get paid."

What? (I probably said it in all caps too!) My mouth probably hit the floor. What do you mean a time sheet? You mean so I can record all ninety hours this week? Do you pay overtime? Overtime sounds great! Thanks!

But I did not say all this—just the *what* part. I found out this was a policy put in place to govern the church employees because there were a few employees (and only a few) who had abused the rules. They were not in the office when they were supposed to be, and rather than address the problem with the few people involved, they created a new rule.

In case you are wondering, I never filled out the time sheet. For a while they hid the practice from me. After six months of insistence (and I mean it was almost a literal fight to do so), we finally dropped the practice for salaried employees. Or at least I think we have.

The point is that policies should be few and effective. When you use a policy to address broad issues or large groups of people when the problem is really a singular issue or involves only a few people, you burden the organization with needless bureaucracy, which only stalls efficiency and frustrates people. This is never good leadership.

4. Never single someone out publicly who has not been talked to privately.

Do I need to explain this one? This pretty much goes back to the Golden Rule. Do not do to others what you would not want done to you.

Even if supervisors needed to sign off on orders—even if I exposed a huge hole in our systems—I should have been talked to privately about my mistake, preferably before the new policy bulletin was released. As you can tell, I learned from the experience. I never again ordered as many collar extenders. (Maybe because we never needed any as long as I was employed there.) Seriously though, it was a good learning experience for me. I would have welcomed a supervisor's addressing the issue with me.

5. *Never punish everyone for the mistake of one.*

Everyone else had to add an unnecessary step to the ordering process because of my mistake. This was unfair to the rest of the team.

When we punish everyone for one person's error, it builds resentment among people who should consider themselves a team. It pits people against one another. At the department store, it caused me to feel uncomfortable for a few days around my peers.

Again, one person's error can help you to discover holes in your systems that need repairing. Good. Fix them. Write better policies if needed. But punishment should always fit the crime and always be applied to the one needing correction.

6. *Never act as if it is not a big deal if you think it is a big deal.*

When my managers talked to me immediately after this incident, they acted like everything was wonderful. I recall one even joked with me when I came to work the day the memo was released—just before I read the memo. Maybe I read more into it than was there, but I felt like people were looking at me strangely as I walked to my department the morning the memo was released. I felt betrayed.

If the problem is a big deal, make it a big deal. And sometimes little things are big deals if they continually occur. For example, I make it a point to never call someone out during a meeting for something minor, such as interrupting others when they talk. I will speak to them after the meeting if it occurs several times. But there have been a few occasions when someone does this repeatedly, even after I have mentioned it to them privately. If I can tell it is disrupting the meeting and annoying others, I will call them out in the meeting. This does two things. One, it lets everyone know you recognize the problem. Second, it puts the person on public notice that you are serious about your correction.

But those are very rare occurrences. Most of the time, minor offenses should be handled for what they are—minor offenses.

7. Never be so weak as a leader that you fail to address the real problem, even if the real problem is a person.

This is a major determining factor of whether or not someone is a leader. Leaders do not shy away from hard conversations. They realize these are necessary for the health of the organization and the individuals involved.

Again, I have seen the church guilty of this. We do not like conflict, especially in the church. But every healthy relationship deals with conflict at times. We simply have to do so in biblical and productive ways.

I am certain I have repeated each of these seven things at times, but the collar-extender experience truly did shape my leadership and management practices. The best thing this experience did for me was give me a principle I have used and often shared with other leaders.

> If you need to slap a hand, bring a
> ruler and show up in person.

To use another word—*lead*. Not because of position or title, but because we need people who can help us get to better places than where we are today. By the way, if you ever need a collar extender I know where you might find one.

You may be wondering a couple of things at this point. First, you may wonder if I am simply an observer of what other people do wrong in leadership. I hope not. I realize we are only in the first chapter, and I have written a lot about the mistakes of others. Although I have shared several poor leadership experiences I have encountered—and I have more to share—I am not bitter. I am not trying to be negative. I am actually a very positive person. I have learned many positive things from others in leadership. As we progress through this book, I hope to share some of those. But we often learn best from the things we do wrong. It is true for me, for others, and it will likely be true for you. I have learned a great deal from other people's mistakes in leadership and others will learn from mine. I certainly hope you will let others learn from yours.

You may also be wondering, if good leadership is not about a position or a title, how would I describe good leadership? It may be helpful to know my basic understanding of what good leadership is as you continue reading.

Years ago, while studying for a master's degree in leadership, I was asked how I would define *leadership*. I have never really come up with a definition of my own. Over the years, I have, however, discovered there are certain characteristics good leaders seem to have in common. I write a lot on my personal blog about this one subject. I am confident we know good leadership when we see it.

Michael Useem, in his book *The Leadership Moment*, offers nine accounts of leaders facing critical moments. While I knew most of the situations in the book, I could not have told you who led in the crises. Some had big titles and positions, most did not, but all of them had something in common: they led through the challenges of life to take people to better realities than they might have experienced without them. Useem commented: "No wonder we remember wartime prime ministers and presidents better than peacetime leaders. Leadership matters most when it is least clear what course should be followed. Our own turbulent times make this an opportune time to examine what others have done when their leadership has been on the line."[1]

To be a leader, you need more than a title. A title will only take you so far. A position may have power attached to it, but power can be used either for good or for evil. To be a leader, you need tenacity. You need strength. You need character. You need to lead even when your natural inclination is to retreat. You need heart. You need many of the qualities and characteristics I have listed here.

But ultimate leadership is proven not by position or title, rather when, by our sacrifice, we help make life better for other people.

AN EXAMPLE OF TRUE LEADERSHIP

A classic example of not needing a position or title to be a leader came when I ran my first and only marathon. I had been a runner for a number of years and completed multiple half-marathons, but doubling the half is harder than I ever imagined. I registered for the marathon months in advance because I knew I would be motivated to run if I had already paid the fee. It also allowed me to set up a training schedule.

As often happens when I schedule something too far ahead, the months leading up to race day were especially busy. I had numerous speaking events, emergencies in the lives of people in the church, and unplanned family activities. I was sick with allergies for a few weeks. I found it difficult to complete my longer runs, which I knew were critical to a successful race. The longest distance I had run was sixteen miles of the 26.2 required. I was told twenty miles was the minimum, so a couple of weeks before the event, I considered pulling out, knowing I was not well prepared. During the week of the race I decided to run, self-coaching myself I could do it.

The morning of the race was rainy and cold, thirty-seven degrees. The normal temperature would have been in the low fifties. I could not have been more nervous about my abilities. I was about eight miles into the race before I felt warm, but by mile twelve the temperature had risen, the rain had stopped, and I was shedding layers. By the time mile fifteen came, I was miserably hot. If you have ever run long distances, you understand.

I was progressing well with few pains and good momentum.

Then I came to mile twenty, and it was as if I had hit a brick wall. I love long runs, but suddenly this was no longer fun. I debated for a mile or two whether or not to walk the rest of the way or stop altogether.

As any marathon runner knows, the ordeal is as much a mental game as it is physical. I had chosen a race that was smaller than most because it was mostly flat. Being smaller meant there were fewer crowds on the sidelines, no bands or cheerleaders. There were long stretches where it was just the road and me. As an introvert, this was one of the things that initially attracted me to the race.

At mile marker twenty-two, I thought there was no choice about continuing. I was done. I could not seem to go any farther. My legs were cramping and I was out of layers to shed. I was beginning to have stomach pains. But more than anything, I had convinced myself I could not finish.

I walked for probably a quarter of a mile with no one around me, front or back. I appeared to be the only one in the race. I had been looking down, exhausted, but something caught my eye. I looked up and saw a Boy Scout coming toward me. He looked to be nine or ten years old. I could not figure out why he was by himself. Normally, I would have been nicer, but I was tired. We were just about to pass each other when our eyes connected, and he shouted, "Keep going! You can do it!"

I am sure this had been his cheer from earlier in the race and he had said it many times, but for me, this was the time that mattered most. As small a gesture as it might seem, his few words were just the motivation I needed to continue. My gait was probably more of a hobble than a run, but I crossed the finish line—and I was doing more than walking. I finished the marathon!

That Boy Scout did not have a position. He was not an official in the race. He had no title. I do not even know his name (wish I did), but he was very much a leader to me. He helped me get to where I wanted to go, even though I didn't think I could get there. He challenged me to be better than I thought I could be. He influenced me to personal achievement. Sounds every bit like a leader to me.

 **MYTH 2**

If I Am Not Hearing Anyone Complain, Everyone Must Be Happy

RIGHT?

I once mistakenly thought so.

I was speaking at a conference when I received an e-mail from someone on the team. I had recently asked her to head a project for a new initiative at our church. I had complete confidence in her. She would periodically update me, but I had given her the reigns to lead this effort.

Then I got her e-mail. The first paragraph said:

You say that when we are frustrated to tell you rather than complain . . . so . . . :-)

I have learned over time that smiley emoji means "I am going to say something difficult, but I want to soften the blow."

Just her opening words motivated me. I wondered who in the world had upset her. I really liked this person. She was a great addition to the team. She never complained. So if some-one had made her this upset, I was going to launch my attack against them.

Not being a detail person, I was about to stop reading and reply back, tell her not to worry, I would handle this. But some-thing told me to continue reading.

> I have been frustrated with the Next Steps process/develop-ment. The long process (taking over a year now) has made it better, and I definitely believe that we are finally ready organizationally and developmentally to launch. I think we have greatly refined mission statements, goals, pur-pose, etc. to most effectively put it out there for people to see and read. AND the process, in my opinion, has greatly improved the information we provide on the website. So I think we've needed a year to really finalize what Next Steps should be.

At this point I was still wondering who she was upset with. And then I read the next line.

> All that said, I have been disappointed with your "presence" in the development process.

Wow! She was upset with me. She went on to tell me how she felt as though I had lost interest and how I was not into the details of the project. Saddest of all, she did not think I cared about the final outcome of a project she had poured her heart into completing.

I was devastated.

And let me tell you, the last part of her assessment was not true. I did care. I cared greatly. The project was initially my idea. I really believed it was going to be one of the best things we had done as a church to help people grow in their faith.

But she was dead-on right: I had abandoned her to the process.

The fact is, I had been traveling a great deal during the time she was working on the project. But I trusted her so much, I did not think I needed to know the details. She did great work and I believed in her. I felt I could simply relegate the project to her and walk away from it until she was done. (And I used the word *relegate* here instead of *delegate* because relegate and delegate are not the same things. Relegate simply means to reassign responsibility, but it implies you are done with the assignment. Delegation requires you to remain close to the project until completion. We will talk about delegation later in the book, which is how I should have assigned the project.)

But in the process of relegating, I left her feeling unvalued. I was wrong to do so, and I felt horrible about it.

Let me pause and say, this was a test of my heart as a leader. I did care. If you have quit caring—or never cared—about the emotional well-being of the people you are trying to lead, you have lost touch with an essential component of leadership. We cannot lead people whom we do not love.

I immediately tried to call her, but she did not answer. I knew it took a lot of courage to send the e-mail. She was probably not ready to talk. So I e-mailed her. I assured her of my support for the project and her personally—the latter was why I had left her alone—but I apologized for making her feel as I did. I admitted it was wrong. We exchanged a few e-mails. Her last e-mail said, "I do feel very valued and appreciated. Thank you for your assurance."

Whew! Crisis averted. But this was such a huge reminder for me. I would hate for a key associate to ever feel this way about my leadership. I am sure I have done so many other times (there may be many other e-mails after the team reads this chapter), and I am thankful for her boldness in letting me know in time to correct myself.

But I should have made her feel throughout the process the way she did when she ended our conversation.

I learned a lot from our exchange. By failing to check in with her periodically, I did not receive feedback from her and she did not receive feedback from me. My false assumption was the silence between the two of us meant everything was okay. It was not. My quietness gave her the false assumption I was not supportive of her work. Far worse, she felt I was not fully supportive of her.

What a blessing the experience turned out to be for me. It could have been much more damaging to the team had she not been brave enough to e-mail me. But there were great lessons learned through it.

The greatest lesson is this: Never assume agreement by silence. Never assume people are on board because they have not indicated otherwise.

This has implications beyond this one example. It impacts every aspect of leadership. The longer I am in leadership, the more I realize I may not always know the real health of my team or organization at any given time—at least as much as others do.

Do not misunderstand. I want to know. But often, because of my position, I am shielded from some issues. Receiving an honest e-mail from a valued associate who is disappointed in your leadership—this is rare.

And because it is so rare, it can be extremely valuable.

I am a pastor, so receiving criticism is not unusual—especially the anonymous kind. Do anything good, make any change, and someone will complain. I have learned, right or wrong, agree or disagree, some would rather complain behind a leader's back than tell them how they really feel.

Some assume the leader already knows the problem. Or they may think he knows but simply has not done anything about it. Others leave or remain quiet rather than complain, often in an attempt to avoid confrontation.

Beyond this chapter's opening example, I have made the mistake many times of believing everything was great in an area of ministry or with a team member when really it was mediocre at best, simply because I was not aware of the real problems in the organization.

It can be equally true that a leader does not know the full potential of an organization. Some of the best ideas remain untapped for the same reasons. People are afraid of their ideas being rejected, so they do not share them. They assume the leader has already thought of it, or they never take the time to share their ideas. I cannot tell you how many times someone has come up to me after an event with an idea they meant to share with me before the event. I often love their ideas and wish I had heard them earlier.

I have also learned that what I do not know can hurt me. And even worse, it can hurt the team. Obviously, there is no way I can know everything the team does or is doing, but especially when people report directly to me, I at least need to be aware of their efforts. When there are projects I have initiated or need to have involvement in, I must show genuine interest throughout the process.

The bigger question of why this conflict occurred with my associate caused me to spend more time reflecting on it even after I felt it was resolved. What caused me to offend her the way I did and really not feel any guilt about it until she approached me? I am fully capable of being offensive. I have moments when I am not the most caring person in the world. Just ask my wife.

But as a follower of Christ and a minister of the gospel, as someone who truly wants to lead well, I hope it is never intentional. I do not set out to offend people. It was an unintentional act to offend her.

So how did it happen? It happened because I violated several principles of leadership. The first one is simple, but let me assure you it is deep.

PEOPLE ARE DIFFERENT

The first principle of leadership I violated was this: people are different. They think differently. They have different desires. Thankfully—many times—they have different ideas. The way they process and share those ideas are different from other people on the team and from the leader.

We will talk more about how to lead different groups of people in the next chapter, but one of the biggest mistakes I have seen leaders make is to forget that not everyone thinks like the leader. I have made this mistake so many times besides the one mentioned above. We assume what we are thinking is what everyone else is thinking.

Wrong.

When I am assigned a project, I probably do not want someone checking in with me as much as my colleague wanted. Part of this may have to do with the amount of experience each of us has in leadership and project management. This was a fairly big project for her at this point in her career. Much of the difference, however, is simply because we are different.

When you fail to remember this principle of leadership— people are different—you frustrate the people you are trying to lead. You get poor performance from the best leaders on your team, and worst of all, your team fails to live up to its potential.

Naturally, we revert to assuming the way we view a situation is the way everyone else does. This is true in all relationships of life. It is true in friendships, parenting, and leadership. I realize you will have a hard time believing I do this now, after reading this story, but I really try to discipline myself to think otherwise.

(Let me pause and say, I am going to use the word *I* a lot in this book. I do not really like the word much in the leadership vocabulary, because a better leadership word is *we*, but I want you to see how I try to be intentional in these areas of leadership—in this case, remembering that people are different.)

The first thing I do is intentionally surround myself with diverse personalities. For example, I try to have good friends who stretch me as a person, even outside of my work. I have some extroverted friends, for example. And I mean some of these friends do not know how to be quiet—ever. But I love them. One friend seems to never need to take a break from talking. He could carry on a conversation with anyone all the time. When we are together, he stretches me. He reminds me that everyone is not introverted as I am.

One of my closest friends is African American. We have been through so much life together. I love him as if he were my own flesh and blood. We have been friends for many years, and we did a radio program together for almost seventeen years. The color of his skin is important because he has a library of experiences I have never had. He has witnessed racism and prejudice and rejection far more than I. Over the years he has helped me see people differently—and probably more like the way Christ views people.

On any church staff I have led, I want different personalities to complement mine. I want people who are different ages, have different backgrounds, and who come from different demographics. Surrounding myself with these people in my personal life helps me welcome it even more in my professional life.

We will all share a common vision if we are on the same team, but we should have some unique approaches to implementing it. Ask yourself, Have I surrounded myself with people who think just like me?

ASK QUESTIONS

The second leadership principle, which I already knew but obviously needed to be reminded of by hearing my associate complain to me, is the power of asking questions. I should have asked her questions throughout the project.

Great leaders ask questions. Lots of them. One of the best things a leader can do is ask the right questions. The leader can often be the last to know where there is a problem or what others are thinking, so asking questions is critical to good leadership.

Personally, I ask lots of questions. I give plenty of opportunity for input before a major decision is finalized. We do reviews of completed projects as a team. I have regular meetings with direct reports. We have frequent all-staff meetings. I end almost every meeting the same way: What question do you have for me? Over time, I believe the team has come to know I am serious about wanting to know the questions they have about any issue.

I periodically set up focus groups for input on various issues. I want to hear from as wide a range of people as possible. I try to consistently surround myself with different voices so I receive diversity of thought. I place a value on hearing from people, especially those who I know respect me and are not afraid to be honest with me.

GREAT LEADERS, GREAT QUESTIONS

I love a quote attributed to Jack Welch: "When you are an individual contributor, you try to have all the answers. When you're a leader, your job is to have all the questions."[1]

Great leaders ask great questions. Lots of them.

Let me share twelve great leadership questions every leader should be asking often:

1. *What can we learn from this?* This is a great evaluation question, especially after something goes wrong. I use this when the team feels less than wonderful about an event or Sunday.

2. *Do you understand what I am asking you to do?* This should be asked every time a project is assigned. I probably asked this to my associate in the example above, which is why I felt comfortable releasing her to the work, but it is always a valuable question in delegation.

3. *How can I help you?* This should be asked periodically and sincerely. I probably did ask this question initially, but I should have asked it throughout the project. It would have shown my interest and willingness to offer my input should it be needed.

4. *What is next?* Great leaders are always asking this question inside and outside the organization. They ask it of themselves and of the people on their team.

5. *Where should we be placing our best energy?* I like to ask this question quarterly or at least twice a year to help plan our goals and objectives for the upcoming season. We sometimes use this question as a part of a staff retreat.

6. *What am I missing or forgetting?* This question can never be asked too often. It is even good sometimes to allow people to anonymously answer this one. Some

people will remain silent in the presence of the senior leader unless they are specifically given an opportunity to provide input. I am not sure there are many planning meetings that happen on the team where I do not ask this one.

7. *How can we do it better next time?* This is another evaluation question after events or special projects. You want to learn from your mistakes and how to capitalize on the things you did well.

8. *What do you think?* I will elaborate on this later, but I use this one anytime someone asks my opinion. I almost never give them my answer first. I have learned they often already have an answer in their mind. They simply want someone to give them assurance or to see whether the leader will agree before they make a decision.

9. *What changes could we implement to make your work life (or your efforts on this current project) better?* This question is always appreciated and is especially needed when a team member begins to feel overwhelmed. You show you value people when you ask this question.

10. *What would you do differently if you had my position?* I like this as an annual question to reflect on the coming year, but it can be helpful anytime. Try this one next time you have a really difficult decision to make.

11. *Are you enjoying your work?* You will get some unique answers to this one, but it should be asked regularly. Sometimes people will reveal some of their future hopes and dreams to you simply because you asked a question. You may help them grow as a leader or as a

person. There is no greater reward in leadership than having this opportunity.

12. *What would you like to ask me but you have not yet had the opportunity?* This is another question for staff meetings or staff retreats. Sometimes they will not ask me the question while they are in the group, but they will e-mail me later because I gave them the opportunity. It is this type of question that probably prompted the courage from the associate who let me know her true feelings.

Questions are so important to the health of a team. As a leader, I want to know—as best as I can—not only what people are saying but what people are really thinking and not saying. I realize, just because of their position and partly because of personalities, some are not going to be totally transparent with me. I try to provide multiple ways for feedback. It is why I periodically allow and welcome anonymous feedback. I even welcome texting or e-mailing me (depending on the size and structure of the meeting) during the meeting. I have found this approach works better for some who may not provide their voice otherwise.

I need to interject here the reason why asking questions is so important. Years ago I had the opportunity to interview Zig Ziglar for my blog. In his later years he had fallen, and it had greatly impacted his short-term memory. He had a wonderful long-term memory, but he tended to repeat himself in a conversation, forgetting what he had just said.

In that two-hour dialogue, Zig probably said a couple

dozen times, "Always give people a reason why, because if they know the why, they won't care as much about the what."[2] This was gold for my leadership!

So the why of asking questions is because not doing so leads to passive-aggressive followers and unaware leaders.

Have you ever heard of passive aggression? The fact is, sometimes the leader is the last to know about a problem. Leadership intimidates some people. At other times, they do not know how to approach the leader, so they complain to others, not the leader. They do not like or know how to deal with conflict. And sometimes the way I am leading dictates who tells me what I really need to know. Not asking enough or the right questions will injure my leadership every time.

This is especially true for newer leaders. They do not know how others will respond.

Let us be honest. Some people get a little buzzed about stirring up controversy and seeing how others respond to it. Unfortunately, passive aggression is also very prevalent in the church.

The reality is that most of the time, when we do not know the true health of the organization, it is because we are leading in isolation. We do not know what could hurt us most. This is being unaware.

LEADING IN ISOLATION

Not long ago I sat with Matt, a new pastor to an established church. He was trying to hold a church together long enough to help it build again. The previous pastor left town after a series of bad decisions—some decisions the church is still finding out about to this day.

I was happy to help Matt acclimate, but in my mind I had more questions for the pastor who flamed out too early, the one who did not finish well, the one who left a church in a state of disarray, struggling to recover.

And, sadly, I see it all the time. The former pastor suffered from the same temptations any pastor faces. As I learned more of what happened, the number-one problem, in my opinion, was that he was leading in isolation. He had no one in his life who knew him well enough to know when something was wrong and could confront him when necessary.

Leading in isolation is displayed in numerous ways to the detriment of the church or organization. There are so many clear dangers in leading in isolation. Below I have listed seven dangers of not knowing the real health of your organization.

1. *Moral Failure*. Without accountability in place, many people will make bad decisions because no one appears to be looking. We are more susceptible to temptation when we are alone.
2. *Burnout*. We are made for community. There is an energy we gain from sharing life with other people. When the leader feels they are alone, the likelihood of burnout, emotional stress, and depression increases.
3. *Leadership Vacuum*. The leader is clueless to the real problems in the organization and is fooled into believing everything (including the leader) is wonderful.

4. *Control Freak.* The leader panics when others question him. He tries to control every decision and does not want to be found out for not knowing all the answers.

5. *Limits Other People.* The leader in isolation fails to communicate, invest, and release, which keeps other leaders from developing on the team. And, therefore, the organization is not prepared when the leader exits.

6. *Limits the Leader.* The isolated leader never reaches her full potential as a leader because she shuts out influences that would actually help her grow.

7. *Limits the Organization.* In the end, the leader who leads in isolation, who does not know the true health of the organization, keeps the organization from being all it can be. The leader sets the bar of how far an organization can go. Bill Hybels said, "Your culture will only ever be as healthy as the senior leader wants it to be."[3] If the leader is in isolation, the organization will be stifled.

Leader, are you living in isolation? Be honest. Do you need to get out of the protective shell you have made for yourself? The future success of your organization depends on it.

I recognize that many pastors of smaller churches feel they have no option but to lead in isolation. You may feel you have no one you can truly trust in your church, and you have isolated yourself for various reasons from others in the community. As hard as it may seem and as great as the risk may appear, you must find a few people to share your struggles with to avoid these dangers.

THE CULTURE YOU CREATE GIVES FEEDBACK ON YOU

There was yet another leadership principle I was reminded of from my associate's e-mail in the chapter opening. *The culture the leader creates impacts the feedback a leader receives.*

I probably should have already said this, but if you are going to welcome input, you have to actually want to hear from the people on the team, even if the information is hurtful to hear initially. I want any team I lead to feel comfortable to walk into my office and challenge my decisions. (Once I know someone's favorite soft drink, I try to keep it in my office refrigerator, knowing it attracts them for frequent visits. I used to keep candy bars in my office, but then our health insurance challenged us to be healthy.) Granted, I want respect, but the team should expect to receive respect equally from me. Knowing what my team is really thinking empowers me to lead them better.

If a leader wants to hear from their team, there has to be a culture in place that allows for expression of thought. There has to be an environment with all leaders that encourages people to think for themselves. This kind of culture does not happen without intentionality. As a leader, I try to surround myself with people sharper than me, but I want all of us to have the same attitude toward this principle of hearing from others. I believe in the power of we. If we want to take advantage of the experience and talents in our church, we have to get out of the way, listen, and follow other people's leads when it is appropriate.

Have you ever spent time assessing your culture? Earlier I mentioned that great leaders ask great questions. I was referring then to questions the leader asks those who are trying to follow, but leaders need to ask themselves great questions also. Questions about their leadership and questions about the culture the leader is creating.

Let me give you some examples of these kinds of questions.

Questions about our culture

How do our people—staff and church—respond to change? How do we address problems when they arise? How do we plan for the future? How trusted is our leadership? How well do we get along as a team? Is everyone here on board with where we are as an organization? The answers are unique to any organization, and I need to know them in order to lead effectively.

Accessibility and temperament of my leadership

Every senior leader is different. Change the leader and you change some of the unwritten rules and dynamics of the team. Am I considered approachable? Is the staff willing to come to me with problems? Would I know if there was a perceived problem in the church? Do other team members trust my leadership? Am I perceived as being accessible? The answers to these questions may shape how I introduce change or make decisions in the future.

Relationship of team members to each other

Is there a friendship or just a working relationship among the team members? How well does the staff participate with one another at work and outside of work? Is conflict acceptable and healthy? Do team members feel they have the freedom to speak freely with each other when in disagreement? Do people respect one another? Is there a silo culture or a common vision everyone is working to achieve? The healthiest organizations have people working together who genuinely like one another. If it is not there, change will be more difficult, people will become frustrated, and effectiveness will be greatly decreased.

Sense of work satisfaction

Are there long-term team members? Do people stay for a paycheck or a false sense of loyalty or are they genuinely excited about being here? Are team members generally happy with the church? Is there any unrest among the team members? Are there unspoken concerns within the organization? Many times, things like this have been formed over years, sometimes even before a leader has been in the position, but it is valuable information for the leader. It may impact the policies or systems you will try to implement.

Reaction to change

Is the way it has always been done changeable? Is change generally accepted or resisted? Who has to initiate change for it to be effective? What is the anticipated speed of change these days? Who needs to know about the change before it can be done? The success of change will be directly related to the answers to these questions and the way a leader responds to them.

Flow of Information

How does communication really happen? What are the circles of influence? Who drives discussion? Who has influence with their peers? What are the expectations regarding the need to know? Communication is key in any organization, so as leaders, we must understand the way it occurs and when it is not occurring effectively.

As a leader, it is important not only to concentrate your attention on what is easily measured, written in a policy manual, or even sometimes spoken. Other considerations may be more important, even though they may never have been expressed formally. I call these the unwritten rules—the way people actually respond to one another, to change, and to leadership. These are often more important in creating culture than the formal policies and systems we implement.

I am not sure I have ever pulled anyone on the team aside and asked them how they are doing and not received some information helpful in better leading them. They might share something personal, some frustration in their work, or some opportunity they have thought about exploring but have not yet had the courage to pursue. One thing I tell the team continually is that I only know what I know. I do not know any more than this. I should empower the team to share with me as the one brave associate did above, but as a leader, I should equally seek to know the things that people will never share for whatever reason. What I do not know can hurt me and the organization or church I am trying to lead.

Let me close by saying, sometimes leaders feel as though all they do is address other people's problems. It could be a personal problem, an issue with a program, someone on the team, or it could be a problem no one can identify—we just know it is a problem. Leaders often serve in the role of problem solvers.

It is frustrating, as a leader, when you feel you have done your best to address a problem, but from the people's perspective, it still exists.

Ever been there?

What if, in the chapter-opening illustration, after I had apologized, my associate had said she was okay, but she really was not? I might have gone on about my business, assumed we were on the same page, and never thought of it again. The real issue would have remained, however. And it would have become exaggerated over time.

Sometimes, as leaders, we think we have fixed a problem, but we do not actually solve it—at least in the minds of others.

Solving a problem is often a matter of perspective.

Consider the following story. My family was eating at a very popular chain restaurant in the Chicago area. It is a wonderful restaurant, a little fancy, and people often stand in line for hours to eat there.

My son, who was probably ten years old or so at the time, ordered milk. When they set the milk down on the table, he noticed a huge fly floating in his glass. He would not drink it.

We called the waiter over and showed him the fly. The waiter simply grabbed a spoon from the table, scooped the fly out, tossed the fly onto an empty plate on the table, and walked away.

Problem solved, right?

This experience remains funny to us today. In no way did we feel this problem was solved. It may have been fixed—there was no longer a fly in the milk, which was our only concern at the time, but the problem was not solved. My son wanted a fresh glass of milk. We decided we were not up for an argument and instead made a funny memory together. We simply ignored it. My son drank water. And we left the restaurant feeling as though we had an unresolved problem at our table.

Our server, on the other hand, believed he had fixed our son's problem. So everything was good. No fly in the milk—no problem. He never apologized or addressed it again but continued serving us.

This story—as silly as it is—reminds me, as a leader, that just because you fix a problem from your perspective does not mean you have solved it in the eyes of those you lead.

Solving a problem is often a matter of perspective. And understanding this principle means a few things.

First, as a leader, whether or not I have solved a problem—or even addressed it in the eyes of some people—may be based more on a person's perspective, their personal interests or desires, or even their emotional investment than it is on some measurable reality.

My work associate had to clearly feel in her heart that I cared for the project on which she was working. It had to be genuine. I needed to understand my error and own it as my fault, not hers.

Second, I should address the problems that need to be addressed. This does not mean I can fix them all. I need to be conscious of that fact. As hard as I may try to solve people's problems, I may never make everyone happy. In fact, the day I make everyone happy, my job as a leader will be complete.

We will not need leaders if everything is already solved. But I do not see this happening anytime soon. (We call this job security.) But if I see a problem, and there is something I can do about it, I should do my best to solve it.

Finally, and most important, I should always attempt to understand the real problem from the other person's perspective. As much as possible, I should discover what solving it looks like in their eyes. At this point, I can determine whether or not I can solve the problem to their satisfaction.

If our waiter had asked, "Do you want a new glass, or should I just scoop the fly out?" he would have learned how to move from fixing the problem to solving it from our perspective. And though we still tipped him (because we are people of grace), his tip could have been considerably larger.

Here again, this is where a leader asks good questions, repeating back what they think they have heard and following up to see how they have progressed toward addressing the real concerns. Sometimes I am able to solve the problem and sometimes not, but either way, everyone should know and agree on what a proper resolution to the problem would be. This keeps me from spending time and resources attempting to fix a problem I can never solve.

 **MYTH 3**

I Can Lead Everyone the Same Way

I HAVE TWO ADULT SONS. THEY ARE BOTH INCREDIBLE young men and very successful in their respective careers. They both have the maturity and moral character I wish I could say I had at their ages. In their outlook on life, their personal values, and even their sense of humor, they are very similar. They were raised in the same home, and in many ways, it is evident they are a product of their upbringing.

If you are a parent, however, you know they are also incredibly different. I once talked to a woman who had over a dozen children. (I do not remember now if she said thirteen or fifteen, but it doesn't really matter at this point.) She told me each of her children was different.

This is a leadership book, so you did not come here for parenting advice, but I will give you some anyway. Knowing your children are different means you cannot discipline them the same way. You need to do what works best for each child.

Our oldest son was very easygoing. He could be corrected with a stern look or a firm conversation. It seemed the more I disciplined him, the more compliant he became. It actually seemed to strengthen our relationship. He appeared to want structure and correction.

The youngest son, well, not so much. If we had a conflict with him, we had best gird our loins for a fight! He is such a great young man now, actually serving in the ministry. And in fairness, he was never a bad kid. He was, however, very strong-willed, especially in his earliest years. To discipline him meant we needed to clearly let him know who was in control. Many times he felt he was, and he would challenge us if we claimed otherwise. The lighter discipline methods we used with the older child never worked with him.

Most parents understand this illustration, but we sometimes do not realize the same principles apply to leadership. You cannot lead the same and expect the best results from everyone you lead.

One of my favorite ways to study the Scriptures is thematically. I will pick a subject or a phrase and simply read everything I can find about it. I have done this several times with the disciples of Jesus. What interesting and diverse characters! Peter was brash and out of the box, willing to step out of the boat and walk on water or cut off the ear of an enemy. Thomas was a skeptic. He would not believe something until it was proven. What about Thaddeus? He must have been very quiet. I have heard preachers label John—who often called himself the disciple whom Jesus loved and whose mother tried to get him a special position in heaven—with an ego problem.

It is interesting to me that Jesus surrounded himself with such a diverse team. Yet Jesus led them all and led them well.

Diversity can be frustrating to leaders, because we tend to expect people to perform as we would perform. But differences can be extremely helpful. When I treat people only like I would want to be treated, when I hold them to expectations I would want to be held to, the team is handicapped. We are held captive by the preconceived ideas I have as a leader. If the organization is limited to my abilities, it is going to be very limited. I am not talking about the Golden Rule (do to others as you would want done to you); I am talking about different ideas, expectations, and desires. If you recognize the need and want to lead people who are different from you—and you should—you will often have to lead differently from how you would wish to be led.

I have learned the myth that "I can lead everyone the same way" is simply not true. It does not work. People are different and require different leadership styles. I am not saying it is easy, but if you want to be effective, you will learn your people and alter your style to fit their personalities.

Someone asked me, "Who has been the most difficult person you have had to lead?" It was a great reflection question. You learn a lot about yourself in answering it. As a leader for over thirty years, I have experienced just about everything you can imagine in leading people.

During my time as a retail department manager, an employee called in sick because her snake was peeling, and the snake got depressed when he shed. She needed to be home to comfort the snake. When I challenged her about her absences, she had her boyfriend bring the snake to work to see her the next day. To complicate matters, the store security guard—a Barney Fife–type character—pulled his gun on the boyfriend and the snake. Customers were obviously alarmed at both sights. This was a new one. I had my hands full. As a result, I have learned not to be surprised at what people you are trying to lead may say or do. People are different.

I have also learned some people are easier to lead than others. Often personalities, experiences, and preferences negatively impact a person's ability to be led effectively. I made a list of some of the hardest people I have had to lead.

The Know-It-All

It is difficult to lead someone who will not listen. They do not think they have a need for what you have to say. They think they know more than you and everyone else. They may or may not, but it makes them very hard to lead. I recently sat with a man who wanted my help in thinking through an issue, but for everything I offered, he had a better story or idea to trump mine. We did not get very far with my helping him.

The Gifted Leader

Do not misunderstand this one. I do not mean these people try to be difficult. And I always welcome this challenge. But these seasoned leaders bring higher expectations for those who try to lead them. I have had some very successful retired pastors in my churches and on staff. Our staff is full of seasoned ministers with more experience in ministry than me. I love having them, and they keep me on my toes! This is a good thing.

The Hypercritical

When someone is always negative, it becomes difficult to lead them, mostly because they sap your motivation. They never have anything positive to add to the team. The glass is always half empty. And the sky is always about to fall. They are draining.

The Wounded

Wounded people are more resistant to being led to something new until after they heal. I have had a number of staff members who came to me injured. I actually love this as a kingdom ministry. I knew that before I could effectively lead them, I had to help them heal from their past.

The Deeply Insecure

Those who lack self-confidence are harder to lead, because they are hesitant to take a risk. The best leadership involves delegation, which causes people to assume responsibility for a task. Insecure people will usually only move when they are given specific tasks to complete. And while good leaders encourage followers, insecure people need constant feedback and assurance, which can be exceptionally time demanding for leaders.

The Change-Resistant

Leadership always involves change. Always. Without change, there is no need for leadership. Those who cling so tightly to the past are harder to lead to something new. There is nothing wrong with tradition or with enjoying the memories of the past. But when someone's love of history prevents them from embracing their future, it becomes difficult to lead them.

Myself

The hardest person to lead is almost always the leader who is trying to lead the team. If leaders always performed as we want others to perform, we would all be better leaders. In fact, most of us would be excellent leaders.

I am sure I have missed something. A friend saw this list and asked me about leading lazy people. I quickly said I do not lead those people for very long.

The fact is, everyone can be difficult to lead at times and during certain seasons. It is what makes leadership fun, right? Seriously, all of these scenarios and types of people serve a role. They can be valuable people to the team. They sharpen our leadership skills and strengthen our organization.

I want to share some lists—tips—I have learned on how to lead different types of people. These are not necessarily hard people to lead, but they bring unique challenges to leadership. I will address some of the more common ones I have experienced. With this portion of the book you can skip over a section if you never have to lead the particular type of person being described. But I would encourage you to skim it and store the information for another day. You will likely run into each of these types of people if you are in leadership long.

STRONG-WILLED PEOPLE

Children like our youngest—strong-willed in their formative years—often never outgrow their tendency to defy authority. It is usually a temperament issue more than a personality issue, and not a rebellion issue.

I am one of those strong-willed types. I was as a child. My parents were divorced for many of my early years (they later remarried), and my single mother did an amazing job raising two sons and a daughter. My mother is one of the most loving and forgiving people I know, so she honestly claims not to remember how defiant I was. I know, however, the nightmares I have of a fly swatter are not based on fantasy. I also know I can be very difficult to lead.

Here are five tips for leading strong-willed people.

1. *Give clear expectations.*

Everyone responds best when they know what is expected of them. This is especially true of those with strong opinions of their own, those of us who are stubborn people. If you have a definite idea of how something needs to be done, and you leave it as an undefined gray area, strong-willed people tend to redefine things their way. Keep the following in mind with strong-willed people: rules should be few and make sense or they will likely be resisted or broken more often.

2. *Allow individual ways of completion wherever possible.*

Once guidelines and expectations are established, allow people to complete them as they see fit. This is important for all of us, but especially for strong-willed people. Hold strong-willed people accountable for progress more than process. They need to know they can make some decisions and have freedom to explore on their own.

This is why I had a love-hate relationship with math in school. I loved doing math, working to find an answer to a problem. In fact, I was pretty good at it. I even served on the math team for a while. But I hated having to solve the problem by the teacher's methods. I realize the teacher needed to make sure I was not cheating, and I knew how to think through a specified process, but I wanted to invent my own process.

3. *Be consistent.*

Strong-willed people need boundaries, but they will test them. They want to know the limits of their freedom. (A WET PAINT sign really means TEST ME.) Keep in mind these people are unusually headstrong. We have even labeled them as strong-willed. They are not going to be the rule followers on the team. Make sure the rules you have—and there shouldn't be too many—are consistent in application. If it is worth making a rule for them, make sure it is worth implementing.

4. *Pick your battles.*

This is huge. Strong-willed people can be the backbone of the team. They can be loyal, dogmatic, and tenacious—all for the benefit of the vision. What leader does not want people with those qualities? But those same qualities can be where the problems start in leading strong-willed people. It is usually best not to cross a strong-willed person over issues of little importance to the overall vision of the organization. If you back them into a corner, they will usually fight back, and it almost always produces unnecessary conflict.

5. *Respect their opinions and individualities.*

Strong-willed people ultimately want to be heard (as all people do). They are not weird because they sometimes seem immovable. But they do resist leadership most when they sense their voice is being silenced. Learn what matters to them and give credence to their opinions, and you will find them to be some of your most loyal teammates.

PEOPLE YOUNGER THAN THE LEADER

In church planting, it seems these were most of the people I led. Other than one staff person, I was by far the old guy on the team. I learned to appreciate the energy and enthusiasm—and even the idealism—younger people added to the team. But there are some challenges with leading a younger generation of people.

Here are some ways to more effectively lead people who are younger than you.

1. *Give them opportunities to grow.*

Even when you may not agree with their ideas, let them try. They may need to experience failure in order to experience their next success. This is likely how you learned. Help them see how they fit into the organization's continued growth. They want upward mobility.

2. *Realize the generational differences.*

Never pretend they do not exist. They affect how we relate to people, change, and technology. Be honest when you do not understand something they do or the language they use. Ask questions. Learn from them. They have relevant and insightful information for the team.

3. *Allow workplace flexibility.*

Just as with strong-willed people, when leading a younger generation, do not let structure control how people complete their work. Allow individuality. Newer generations aren't as tied to an office as older generations, for example. Let them figure out their how—and often their where—of work progress.

I have found office hours are not nearly as important as progress toward predetermined goals and objectives. For the most part, if the work is getting done well, I couldn't care less how and when it was done.

4. Limit generational references.

The younger generation does value your wisdom. They want it, but they are less likely to be excited about gleaning from us if we always start everything we say with "When I was your age . . ." In fact, avoid continually reminding them how young they are.

5. *Value their opinions.*

It appears the most successful innovations usually come from the younger generation. Who knew Facebook would become such a powerhouse company? Mark Zuckerberg was twelve years old when he became a computer programmer, and he began Facebook from his college dorm room. Do not dismiss their input because you feel they lack experience. They usually are not limited by all the reasons you think something will not work. Who knows? The thing you tried yesterday that did not work just might work this time.

6. *Give them a seat at the leadership table.*

This is perhaps most difficult for some older leaders, because they often gained their position through years of hard work. You may have gotten to your position thanks to years of sweat equity. You may not feel the younger generation has completely earned their seat at the table. But younger generations want leadership opportunities now. We can certainly resist this, but someone will be giving them the opportunity to lead, and we will miss out on their input and involvement if we don't.

The bottom line in leading younger generations is to help them achieve their goals and ideas, not put a damper on them. The value we get is to become people builders, and we gain the energy and enthusiasm of youth.

PEOPLE OLDER THAN THE LEADER

As I said in chapter 1, I was placed in my first paid leadership position almost by default. The department manager left unexpectedly, and I was already there and eager to lead. Everyone working for me was older than I was, including a man who was in his sixties.

Even though I have aged considerably since then and have years more leadership experience, I continue to have positions where people older than me, with more experience than I have in many areas, report to me.

In fact, in the church I currently pastor, I did not only inherit people with more experience, I recruited them deliberately. I do not believe we would have had the success in revitalization we have had without their input. We needed—and continue to need—younger voices on the team, but these seasoned leaders have helped navigate major change in ways I could not have done on my own.

I alluded earlier to our church plant and an older staff member. I intentionally recruited this staff member, who is almost fifteen years older than I. This meant there were literally three generations of leadership in our church plant. I have learned this is unusual for most church plants, but it has proven to be gold for our organizational structure. I cannot testify to this fact for sure, but I have often wondered if a reason we were one of the fastest growing churches in the United States for several years had to do with this diversity in age and experience. It can certainly be more challenging to lead people with more experience than you, but I highly recommend it.

I can tell you without reservation, your leadership will be better if you learn to lead people older—and wiser—than you are today. And do not be afraid to recruit them.

Here are some tips for leading people older than you.

1. *Recognize the difference.*

As with leading people younger than you, there will be generational differences. When a person is ten, twenty, or even thirty years older, they likely have different needs and expectations from their leader and the organization. They may need different benefits, different work schedules, and even different leadership styles, depending on their age and stage of life. You should maximize your leadership by adapting your style to the person you are leading anyway, but this will be especially true when you lead someone who doesn't always need as much of your leadership.

2. *Give credit for wisdom earned.*

This is key. If you do not recognize and value the fact that age and experience has given them something you may not have, you will never effectively lead someone older than you. Most likely there will naturally be things the other person has experienced that you have not yet experienced. Do not let this intimidate you. Allow it to work for you by gleaning from their wisdom.

3. *Stand your ground respectfully.*

If you are in the position to lead, do your job. Those older than you were probably raised in a generation where they expect you to lead, but as you should with any person you lead, be respectful. If someone is older, most likely they will be more sensitive to a disrespectful younger leader and react negatively. They may not say anything, because this may be part of their culture, but you will not have their respect if you are not leading with respect.

4. *Learn from them.*

Be honest when you do not know how to do something, such as handling difficult issues or people. If the older person knows how, let them show you. It is okay that you have some things to learn. We all do. The older a person becomes, the more in tune they become with the fact that no one knows everything. Ask good questions. "Have you ever experienced something like this before in your leadership?" "What would you do if you were in my shoes?" "Am I missing anything, in your opinion?"

I would have flopped in my first leadership position had the man old enough to be my grandfather not invested in me personally. He passed away a few years ago, but I am incredibly indebted to him.

5. *Be clear on expectations.*

More than likely a person from another generation is more accustomed to structure than you are. There were days past when expectations were more clearly defined and people knew what was expected, and they welcomed the structure. Organizational charts were more linear. Job titles meant more about what a person did on the team. Be aware of this. You do not necessarily have to change your leadership style to accommodate this expectation, but you do need to recognize and understand when they may need a little more clarity on your expectations. Out of loyalty (a valuable trait), they may wait until they know for sure you want them to move forward on a task or project.

6. *Do not play games with them, even if you are intimidated.*

I have seen this many times. An older team member intimidates the leader, so they dance around an issue or fail to handle conflict. The leader might make excuses for not knowing something or pretend they have more experience than they actually have with an issue.

People with life experience can usually see through that type of behavior. Age and maturity will make them less intimidated by you. Be kind. Be respectful always, but be direct. Shoot straight with them. Stand firm when needed. The fact is, older team members will probably have handled worse situations than the one with which you are challenging them. They will welcome your secure leadership if it is handled appropriately.

7. Be patient with them.

This is changing rapidly, but sometimes older team members may not be as culturally, technologically, or trend savvy. They may need a different form of communication, or you may need to explain something in a different context. But they will make up for it by adding to the team in other ways. Be prepared to allow extra training for them if needed, even in some things that appear basic for you.

There were many times in business when I would have never made it without someone helping me who had more experience. This is still true today. I continue to surround myself with mentors in life and church.

Granted, if the person is cranky, rigid, or troublesome, do not add them to your team. But these people can exist in all generations.

When you shy away from someone for your team because they are older or more experienced than you, you ignore some of the hardest working and dedicated team members. And the humility in knowing you are leading people wiser than you will make you a better leader.

CREATIVE PEOPLE

I love creativity. In church planting, we surround ourselves with highly creative minds and allow them to dream big dreams. One thing I realized early in the life of the church, however, is that creative people can be more difficult to lead. They do not always fit within the established systems of the organization.

For clarity, in case my tone about creative people sounds degrading, I want you to know I am not anti-creative people. I am actually a creative myself, not an artistic creative, but an idea creative. And these are true for me too.

If you want to lead creative people without stifling their creativity, here are some needs they have that I have observed help them to thrive.

1. *Clearly defined parameters of whatever you are trying to attain.*

I used to think when leading creative people, the key was to free them to create. I have learned—the hard way—freedom alone for a creative person can spell disaster. Nothing gets accomplished. No one is happy. We falsely assume creative people only need freedom in order to create, and they do, but they need more. They need clear lines of direction, a clear vision. It helps them to build a box around a certain end goal or objective. They do not like to be held to standards they do not know exist or put into a set of rules or a script of how to attain the vision, but they want to know what is expected of them in advance.

2. *Accountability along the way.*

Creative people need someone to check in with them periodically. They often need motivating. They tend to thrive on encouragement. Let them know if they are making progress toward the goal, and point out to them when they are not. Some creative people struggle with follow-through, so give them a target date and hold them to it as much as possible.

3. *Find the structure that works for them.*

Creative types need and want appropriate boundaries—not too constricting—but they are often not good at developing those boundaries for themselves. Without the lines, without the accountability, creative people do not flourish. They flounder. Things are not creative. They are messy. Creative people love freedom, but it works best when it is sandwiched between clarity and structure.

4. *Freedom to draw within the lines.*

This is a freedom creative people love. They want limited micromanagement and maximum empowerment. They need to know they have the freedom to dream and to fail. Again, all of this is within broad, very broad, but defined boundaries.

5. *Ready forgiveness.*

Creative types often are messy people when trying to explore new ideas, and they make mistakes along the way. Recognize this as part of what makes them successful at what they do. You have to exhibit lots of patience with creative types. They do not always fall within an established system, but remember this is one reason you want them on your team. They help to take you places you would not go otherwise.

6. *Reward and praise often.*

Everyone needs to feel appreciated, but highly creative people tend to thrive on it. It stirs their creative energies. They like to know you admire their work.

This next one is jumping into deeper water of leadership, but it is probably among the most frequent questions I receive.

Bob, a student pastor, serves with a very demanding, hard-to-read pastor. He loves the church and his students, but he is trying to decide if he can stay. If Bob has any chance of influencing his pastor, much depends on how the student ministry is led. The pastor has thwarted every change Bob has tried to implement.

How do you lead people who are supposed to be leading you?

LEADING THE LEADER

Have you heard the term *leading up*?

Here are seven suggestions:

1. *Give lots of respect and understanding.*

You may actually know more than the person leading you about a particular subject or issue, but chances are they have experience you lack. They are in the leadership position for some reason. Even if you do not agree with their being the leader, there is something to be gained simply from sitting where they sit. Everyone likes to be respected for their experience and position.

Keep in mind some of your leader's experiences may have been negative and may have prompted the style of leadership they provide now. Try to put yourself in their shoes. If you have any hope for the leader's approval, you will need to show you respect the position of authority that person has in the organization and you are at least attempting to understand the pressure they are under as a leader.

I am not suggesting this is easy, but it is vital to gaining the trust of the leader. I am also not suggesting you falsely maneuver your way into the leader's inner circle. I am suggesting you humbly and genuinely give credence to the leader's position. (I have already covered the myth that a position makes one a leader, but keep in mind, many people still believe it.)

2. *Demonstrate commitment to the leader and the organization.*

Loyalty is such a rare thing in today's work environment; it is refreshing to a leader when we find it. Buy into the vision and the direction of the team, and make your support known in word and action. It will impress those around you and the leader. This is demonstrated over time, not simply when you need something.

3. *Do good work.*

This should go without saying, but have a good work ethic. Produce more than you're expected to. You do not have to sacrifice your family on the altar of work, but you may have to be more disciplined in how you do your work in order to be more productive. Again, it is a rare commodity today when someone tries to do more than is required of them. When a leader spots someone willing to go the extra mile, that person gains approval and recognition.

4. *Display kindness to everyone around you.*

This is a general principle when working with others, but it is especially true in this situation. Too often, when we are not happy with leadership, we let it be known by how we treat others. If you are not likable to the leader—or to others on the team—they are going to respond likewise. Even if the leader is unkind at times, attempt to win them over with kindness: "A soft answer turns away wrath, / But a harsh word stirs up anger" (Prov. 15:1). Treat them as you would want to be treated. It is your best opportunity to influence them.

For example, we had someone on the team who would rarely speak to me in the hall. When she did acknowledge me, it was quick and simply responsive. There was no real engagement beyond what conversation had to take place. I knew she had a reputation of being quick-tempered, though she never expressed this to me personally. I try to be visible to the team and engaging, because I know there's value in this as a leader. But with this person, I gave up trying. She was not very kind. How successful do you think she would be in trying to lead me should she have chosen to do so?

5. *Acknowledge past accomplishments.*

Recognize the leader's previous and current contribution to the organization as well as their wisdom. Even if you genuinely respect a leader, they will not likely know or appreciate the respect until you let them know it personally. When a leader feels appreciated for their previous efforts, they are less likely to feel threatened and more likely to welcome input into future decisions.

6. *Be inquisitive of the leader.*

Most likely the leader has something from which you can learn. Request the leader's input and help, even if you do not necessarily need it. Be genuine, and it will show that you value them. Everyone likes to be recognized for their accomplishments. The best leaders gain insight from lots of different sources. Model this for the ones who are leading you. You may not see the relevance of their insight right now, but they may actually surprise you and add something from their experience you have not thought of or been exposed to yet.

7. *Partner with them.*

This is huge if you want to influence—lead—those who lead you. Find areas of common connection. Even if there is a significant age gap or different paradigms of life, there will be many things you have in common. This is part of networking and team building. I see many younger leaders who only want to hang out with younger leaders, and vice versa for older leaders. This will never bridge the generational gap, and this is not healthy for the organization. It certainly will not help you lead up if you exclusively associate with people in your stage of life or at your organizational level on the team.

Those are a lot of suggestions. There are certainly others I could have included, but this is a start. The point is that you must think through strategically who you are leading and what will be most effective in leading them to their full potential.

The question you may be wondering now is who fits where in this discussion of leading people different from you. Let me offer the following suggestions.

Know your team.

This is true when they are paid or volunteers. People are more likely to develop trust in people they know. Depending on the size of the organization, you may not be able to get to know everyone intimately, but you should certainly know those you directly supervise. I have found I am not very effective if I have more than three to five direct reports, but it is important I know them beyond the work environment. This is not to say you cannot learn things about a broader group within the organization, but you may have to rely on others or other means to get to know them as well.

We use assessments such as Myers-Briggs[1] personality inventory, StrengthsFinders,[2] and DiSC[3] personality test. These tests help me to discover the personalities and hidden skills I may not have known otherwise. It also helps to know the holes in your team and to pinpoint what types of people are not represented.

Whenever I accepted a position with an established church, we conducted the Myers-Briggs assessment for all staff members. I learned we had a lot of very structured, detail-oriented people and very few creative types. (It was probably one of the reasons our operating policies manual was almost a hundred pages long.) As a result, when we added people to the team, we sought out some out-of-the-box, random thinkers.

We also have lots of brainstorming sessions in which people are free to express themselves. Our staff meets regularly, and we intentionally get away for retreats. If we go out of town, we bring our spouses for accountability purposes and so we can get to know them also.

Be intentional.

A leader never learns their team and their differences unless they value the importance of doing so and intentionally set out to do it. I do a lot of walking in the halls. I find people are more likely to talk to me if I am not in my office. A chance meeting at the copier can be one of the best ways to get to know people.

The first year I was in a new church, I kept an individual Evernote file on each staff member. It sounds a little creepy now. They did not know it then, but they will when they read this book. My purpose, though, was to jot down observations about them as I was learning about them. These notes included the assessment tests they had taken, their likes and dislikes, and sketches of my encounters with them. If I want to remember something, I need to write it down. This practice helped me to learn about the people I had been called to lead. I knew we would never be successful at our revitalization efforts unless we were a healthy team. I certainly could not do it alone. And this required that I know the team I would be leading.

Continually practice leadership development.

One of the best ways to get to know your team is to make it part of your leadership development. The more diversity on a team, the more leadership development becomes important. You are not trying to change people, but you are trying to make sure everyone is on the same page as far as the vision you are attempting to attain. This requires consistent development.

I hear leaders say they cannot afford leadership development. I understand the concern. Development can be expensive. I have operated in very small contexts where budgets were stretched simply to keep the electricity bill paid. When budgets are stretched, development is often pushed to the back burner or cut altogether from the budget.

When I arrived at an established church, I found it had been going through several years of decline in giving. Thus they basically cut out all development activities from the budget. This is dangerous for a team that wants to remain healthy and growing.

If a team is not learning and improving, it will soon struggle to attain any level of success. But leadership development does not have to be expensive, and you learn a lot about your team in the process. It is important, therefore, to find ways to develop even with stressed budgets.

The following are ten inexpensive or less expensive ways to offer development to a team.

1. *Bring in a leader.* It may be cheaper to bring the expert to you than it is to attend a conference. Find someone from whom your team can learn and pay their expenses to visit the team. We have found there are great leaders in our city, either leading a business or a nonprofit, who bring valuable insight to the team. The team actually learns better when they are hearing good leadership principles from multiple sources.

2. *Send a representative.* You may have to draw names to decide who will go, but pay for one person to attend a conference with the catch that they have to bring information back to share with the team.

3. *Read a book together.* The number of available leadership books easily outnumbers the months a team will be together. Find some good ones and read and digest them as a team. Assign one person each chapter, and allow them to lead a discussion of the content.

4. *Use local resources.* Most likely there are large businesses or universities within driving distance that have development offices or procedures to develop people, with skilled people who can inexpensively invest in your team. I have found that they're willing to share what they have learned with small groups, such as a church team.

5. *Online or teleconference.* Technology allows for some great online conferences. Gather the team around a computer and learn without leaving the office. Additionally, if you have a telephone, you have another great way to connect with other leaders. Arrange for a conference

call with one, and let the team ask questions and process the interview together.

6. *Pool your resources.* Join forces with another church or similar business to accomplish any of these ideas. Learn from each other. Swap responsibilities to lead a development activity. Share the costs of bringing in a speaker and do a combined mini-conference of your own.

7. *Visit organizations similar to yours.* We encourage the staff to visit other area churches, either individually or as a group. Sometimes the quickest ways to promote change is to introduce leaders to other environments. It is a great way to develop new ideas and improve on what you are doing as you see what others are doing firsthand. Be sure everyone goes with the expectation of bringing something back to the team.

8. *Learn from each other.* Chances are good that everyone on your team has something to offer that can make the team better. Take turns sharing with one another something you already know or are learning.

9. *Scavenger hunt.* Assign each team member the task of finding the best development idea and sharing it with the rest of the team. Whether online, in a book, or through networking, seek out new ideas and improvements you can share with the team. The process of sharing ideas will prove to be development.

10. *Trial and error.* The best development may be to put systems in place that allow the team to take risks and then evaluate the success or failure in order to learn from them and grow. Teams should be doing this anyway, but

teams often fail to intentionally learn from the process of doing normal work.

Development does not have to be expensive, but it needs to be done. In doing so, you will learn a lot about the people on your team.

CULTURAL DIFFERENCES

As I was completing this book, I began studying some of Erin Meyer's work on understanding cultural differences in working with people, especially in a global context. Our church is attracting more internationals, and this is becoming an important topic for us. I do not have time to explore it here, but it opens a whole other issue in understanding people and how it impacts leadership today.

In her book *The Culture Map*, Meyer wrote: "Yes, every individual is different. And yes, when you work with people from other cultures, you shouldn't make assumptions about individual traits based on where a person comes from. But this doesn't mean learning about cultural contexts is unnecessary. If your business success relies on your ability to work successfully with people from around the world, you need to have an appreciation for cultural differences as well as respect for individual differences. Both are essential."[4]

In short, we have to continually learn about the people we are trying to lead, because we are in the people business.

When I was in retail business, I had an employee who

went through a period of several weeks during which she was very rude to our customers. She had been a good employee, but something changed. Of course, in retail, the way you treat customers determines whether or not they return. Customer service can make or break a business's success.

Although I was a young leader, I knew I had to address her rudeness with her, and I did so on several occasions. She never made any excuses. She apologized and said she would improve. But she did not. Since the problem continued, I felt I needed to address it more seriously.

When I was about to fire her, someone shared something with me about this person. Namely, she was struggling with some incredible pressures at home. Consequently, whenever she had a difficult customer, her emotional state caused her to react in an equally difficult way. It was not right, and it could not continue, but at least I knew why it was happening. Instead of firing her, I actually helped her through these issues. We saved a valued employee.

This taught me an important principle in working with people: consider a person's heart before considering their actions.

It is not only the right thing to do and a good leadership principle, but it is actually a God-like attribute. When God set out to look for a king to replace Saul, he told the prophet Samuel, "For the LORD does not see as man sees; for man looks at the outward appearance, but the LORD looks at the heart" (1 Sam. 16:7).

As much as I can—as a pastor, a leader, a customer, a friend—I try to consider what could be going on in a person's life before judging their behavior. This helps me to lead. This helps me to care. This helps me to pray. This helps me to respond in a loving way.

This works with employees, waitresses, family, and friends. It changes my attitude even if it does not change theirs. And many times, the way I respond determines the way they respond.

There are still times when people are simply rude. They simply underperform expectations. Those situations still need to be addressed. This is part of leadership also. But understanding a person's heart helps you to address the real issue rather than simply address the symptoms. Even when there are deeper issues, there will be times a person simply is not a fit for the position. But at least you will have attempted to understand and address the real problem.

I try to remember that all people have injuries. They have stories. Their actions are often indicative of their stories. Knowing the story behind their actions will often alter your response to their actions.

I began with an illustration about how different our boys are from each other. Imagine if I had not taken the time as a parent to understand their unique personalities, their individual gifting, or their separate desires. We would have had both boys playing soccer or baseball when each of them likes one and not the other.

I found my best way to get to know them was when a ball was in play. My best opportunity for teachable moments was when I invested the time in them to play their favorite sport. Again, I would have missed half of these opportunities—or only had them with one child—had I not understood this about them.

It is the same way with the teams we lead. If we believe

knowing the people we lead and their individualities is important—and we should—then we will make the extra effort to do so.

Lee was one of the most difficult people I ever led. He had one of those sharp mouths and you never knew when you were going to be the recipient. It did not seem to matter if you were the senior leader; if Lee thought it, you would hear it.

I have pretty thick skin, but there were a few times my feelings were hurt when Lee challenged me. I was seasoned enough to not let him know he had gotten to me, but somehow I think he knew. Lee was so talented that I did not want to lose him. But there were some days I questioned if it was worth it to keep him.

One day I decided to get to know him. Cheryl and I went to dinner with Lee and his wife. I then started to find reasons to visit his office. We went to lunch together. At first it was a chore, but over time it became easier. I found out I really liked Lee. And Lee had a story. He had been treated very poorly by past leaders and was very guarded where the senior leader was concerned. He was reacting to me out of pain, not personality.

This insight changed everything! I could work with this. My job became less about trying to work with Lee and more about trying to identify with Lee and earn his trust. The intentionality paid off big time. Lee proved to be one of my best hires. I would put him on any team I was leading today. I would not have known this had I not taken the time to get to know him.

Who on your team are you struggling to lead? Could it be you can't lead them well because you don't know them well enough—yet?

 **MYTH 4**

Leadership and Management Are the Same Thing

I WAS WORKING WITH THE BOARD OF A CHRISTIAN NON-profit as they began their search for a new executive director. The organization had experienced a decade of instability and decline. They wanted to grow again. They wanted to renew their vision and see vibrancy return to the organization.

They had gone through several executive directors during the time, and none had stayed very long. So they had two concerns: They wanted to figure out why the turnover was so high in the executive director position and why they could not grow as an organization. They felt the two were related.

During our talks, they kept using the term *leader* in describing the type of individual they wanted for a new director. They indicated leadership had been a strength of their last few directors, and yet they did not grow. They assumed the director did not stay long enough to generate the results they were seeking. What was the problem? What were they doing wrong in finding a director? This was my baseline question.

I had to discern some of the culture in order to answer their original question. After further talks, I did not know definitively why the previous directors left. There could have been many reasons, but in listening to their vision, hearing what they wanted in a director, and uncovering the culture of the organization, it was fairly easy to diagnose their problem. They were saying one thing but behaving differently whenever a new director was selected.

They recruited someone in order to lead them to grow again, but the board exerted control over the director any time the director actually tried to lead. They resisted change. They did not give the director hiring and firing privileges over the staff. They were never willing to take risks in the budget in order to explore new opportunities.

I told them: "You do not want someone to lead. You want someone to manage."

Organizations do it all the time. Often we hire a leader when we really want a manager, and vice versa. When we do, there is a misfit between culture and expectations.

The truth is, this organization did not want an executive director to lead them toward a renewed, even God-given vision. They wanted a person to manage the complicated and man-made operations they already had in place. I was not trying to be cruel but to help eliminate future disappointment by letting them know in advance what they were looking for in a new person.

This happens in churches all the time. Expectations are placed on the pastor to lead, but when they actually do, they face a resistant, almost surprised audience. And the reality is, the church does not want a pastor to lead; they want a pastor to manage the church as it already is—and often has been for years.

> Leaders lead change.
> Managers guide systems.

Simply put, leadership is more about empowerment and guiding people to a common vision, often into the unknown. Management is more about maintaining efficiency toward a predetermined destination.

This, in my opinion, was the organization's problem in keeping a director. They did indeed find leaders, but they expected them to be managers. During our discussion, it became apparent to me the previous directors were quickly warned by the board—or discovered the hard way—what could not be touched. They were handed stacks of policies. They were directed toward the path of continuity. The board assumed the organization would grow if current structures, which had worked previously, were managed well.

In any organization, it is important to know the difference. Do you want a leader or a manager?

As I told this board, I am not pretending it will be easy to go the leader route. It is the more uncomfortable choice. There will likely be tense times at board meetings. Staff and volunteers will be stretched. Things may even be miserable at times. Change is hard. The fact is, managing existing structures and systems can often (but not always) be easier than leading toward something new.

My advice to them was to change what they were doing (how

they allowed a director to lead) in order to get what they claimed they wanted. They would have to decide what they wanted after the hire even more than before the hire. The expectations they placed on the director after they arrived should make a difference in who they were looking for in a new director. And this was the harder part of the discussion: they might need to change how they operated as an organization and as a board, as well as what they were willing to do to embrace change, before hiring the next director. Determining who they wanted and what they wanted them to specialize in were key before recruiting someone to do the job.

It was a difficult conversation. I am not sure it was what they wanted to hear, but it was definitely what they needed to know. Thankfully it ended well. They had not asked for my management expertise; they asked for my leadership advice.

If you want someone to take what you already have and keep it running, get a manager. The best you can find. Make sure they have a pure heart, good intentions, and great training. Make sure they fit with the culture and believe in the vision. Then let them go to work in maintaining what you currently have. You will be happy, and they will be happy.

If you want someone to take you to new places, even better places than you have been before, then you need to find a good leader. And let them lead. Get behind them and support them privately and publicly, and then hold on tight, because it's going to be a bumpy ride. You can celebrate the new when it comes.

The problem for the practice of management is it naturally deals with an element of control, which is often viewed as a negative. Read the latest books and blogs on organizational health (including mine). It is popular to talk negatively about control issues. Leader types (like me) often rebel against any mention of control in favor of releasing people to dream and explore. Leadership and management are not the same thing, but we need both.

In their book *Reviewing Leadership*, Robert Banks and Bernice M. Ledbetter wrote:

> Leadership and management are two distinct yet related systems of action. They are similar in that each involves influence as a way to move ideas forward, and both involve working with people. Both are also concerned with end results. Yet the overriding functions of leadership and management are distinct. Management is about coping with complexity—it is responsive. Leadership is about coping with change—it too is responsive, but mostly it is proactive. More chaos demands more management, and more change always demands more leadership. In general, the purpose of management is to provide order and consistency to organizations, while the primary function of leadership is to produce change and movement.[1]

I have seen churches confuse these two functions. And it goes both ways. I have seen the following scenario many times. When the pastor leaves—especially if things have not been going as well as people would like them to be going—the church blames it exclusively on poor leadership. So they recruit a pastor who they believe excels in leadership. Their interviews are heavy with leadership questions. They check references to see what kind of leader they wanted. They find a leader, when they're really looking for a pastor who can manage a church full of good leaders.

Other churches are like the nonprofit mentioned earlier. They say they want a pastor who will lead, but when the pastor arrives, the church does not allow the pastor to lead. They refuse change, preferring things the way they have always been.

And still other churches—this may be true especially in church plants—resist management all together. They want to be as free as the Spirit of God leads (which they should be), but they never develop any systems and procedures that allow for healthy growth for the church in the years to come. Again, every organization needs both: leadership and management.

There will be some who will need to read this paragraph again. Every person on every team does a little of both leadership and management, and we certainly need good leadership and good management. In fact, we have almost created a culture where the term *management* has a negative connotation. Organizations do not always look for people with good management skills anymore. They look for leaders. It seems unpopular or unappealing to say, "I'm a manager." Instead, we want to hear someone say, "I'm a leader."

This mind-set is dangerous. We still need good management. That's worth repeating: we still need good management.

In organizations today, leadership has overpowered management as the preferred function. I have to be honest, I feel more qualified to talk about leadership than I do management. I am a better leader than I am a manager, but the reality is that good leadership includes a healthy dose of good management and vice versa. Both disciplines are equally important for a healthy organization, including the church. We have to make sure both are covered in the organizational structure.

But they are not the same thing.

THREE FUNCTIONS IN EVERY ORGANIZATION

Several years ago I read Raymond P. Rood's article "How Then Should Organizations Live?" He makes the point that every organization has three basic needs. This philosophy resonated with me, and based on my experience, I can see how it relates to churches, businesses, and nonprofits. The following are the three things Rood says every organization needs.

Growth

Rood wrote, "Growth needs focus on productivity and expansion." The growth of any organization is vibrant and fast-paced and requires lots of energy and attention. Growth is a world of numbers and percentages of increases. Without growth, an organization will eventually die, but if an organization only grows and never matures, growth will not sustain itself for long.[2]

We experienced this in a church plant. Most of us had come from established churches, and we, candidly, were somewhat rebellious against rules, policies, and procedures. But the more we grew, the more it became obvious to us that we needed all of them. Which leads to the next need of every organization.

Maintenance

According to Rood, "Maintenance needs focus on order and the reduction of problems." The more an organization grows, the more it needs a structure in place to manage the growth. This structure is what Rood calls *maintenance*. This is where you develop systems and procedures. Organizational rules come into play with this function. You formalize the things you want to continue to do well. Good maintenance is critical to sustaining growth.[3]

Some people love the maintenance world. They love to create and abide by structure. Good managers thrive here. Maintenance is extremely necessary for the organization to remain healthy. Still, if all an organization does is maintenance, it will become dull, boring, legalistic, uninspiring, and it will eventually die. (Did I paint that picture well enough?) Some organizations and even churches die because they live exclusively in the maintenance world. I have especially noticed this in established churches. They become a large bureaucracy of rules and regulations, designed with good intentions to sustain the organization's growth, but without the other two functions, the structure of the organization begins to strangle them.

I have been blessed by God to serve in some fast-growing churches. We received recognition as both a church plant and an established revitalized church as one of *Outreach* magazine's one hundred fastest-growing churches. I could write another chapter on the blessings and curses of growth. The maintenance function played an equally important role in both.

In church planting, we often lack enough structure to

sustain our growth. In established churches, we often have to destroy some of our policies and procedures to encourage growth. This leads to the third basic need of organizations.

Development

Rood wrote, "Development needs focus on organizational quality." The development needs of an organization are designed to take it to the next level of success. This is where an organization really matures and improves. Development generates lasting principles and values and prepares an organization for years of growth and success. Here, too, the lack of development will doom an organization to eventually wither and die.[4]

A common mistake is to confuse development with growth. Growth is always growth. It is primarily focused on things getting bigger. We need this function. Development, however, is focused on improvement—some of which may or may not lead to growth. This may be completely internal development. For example, developing an employee retention plan. It could possibly lead to future growth, but this is not the immediate intent. Keeping valuable employees is the goal.

Another example would be the development or improvement in internal accounting or paperwork systems, that is, the maintenance function. Again, it is more difficult to tie these directly to growth sometimes, but they can always be tied to development.

As much as I love growth, I really am a development person. I always hope this leads to growth, but improvement is my main objective.

For an organization to thrive it must perform all three

functions well. Using Rood's information, I have expanded my thinking around these areas and discovered a few things that have been helpful to me in leading and managing the team.

First, I have learned that everyone in the organization tends to prefer one of these three functions, even though we need all three to be successful in our roles. For a position to be successful, it should have a primary focus on one of these three functions, although, again, all of them are necessary at some level for every position.

If a person is mismatched in one of these functions, they will be more susceptible to burnout. A person with a preference for growth or development, for example, will burn out sooner if they are asked to work primarily in the maintenance function. (Please do not place me in a strictly maintenance position.)

We have to discipline ourselves as leaders and team members to make sure all three functions are a part of our work and organization.

This is the harder one, but I have learned the higher you go in an organizational structure, the more you are expected to lead, the more time you will need to spend on the development function.

I frequently walk teams through these functions in a retreat setting. We expand our thoughts on these three needs as they relate to the life of our church and the individual areas in which we serve. The discussion always leads to ways we can improve in each function. As a pastor and a leader knowing the importance of these functions, I want to make sure we are excelling in all of them.

I have heard people say they love all of these, and a few overly confident people say they are good at all three of them. I question this. In my experience, they may enjoy elements of all of them, and may even be good at all of them to some degree, but there will be one preference in the bunch. Similarly, there will be one that is a weakness for them.

For years I thought I was good at maintenance because I like organizational efficiency. I like to see things work well. I use a lot of checklists. When I was placed in a position where I did maintenance almost exclusively, I bombed out.

When shaping a team, we need to make sure that people specializing in all three functions are represented and each are allowed to lead in their area of strength.

I know now that I'm a development guy. My lesser strength is in maintenance (bombed out, remember), but I have seen what happens when the team is weak in this area. I love the growth area, being a starter and an entrepreneur. But in an established organization, I tend to drift toward development, which often involves starting something new in the organization. If development were all I had to do, I would be happy. To be an effective leader, however, I must discipline my time to focus on all three needs. I can specialize in one, but I must be committed to playing a part in each.

Rood uses the term *maintenance*. I call it *management*. And there are several different areas of management we need to consider.

TIME MANAGEMENT

Time management is simply making sure we have time to do what needs to be done. The larger a church gets or the more leadership responsibility God calls me to, the greater the tension I feel between being available and being accessible. And I have learned—in order to be effective, to protect my family, and to avoid burnout—I cannot always do both.

Truth be told, there are too many demands on my time to always be available. Sometimes there are more requests for my time than hours in the day. Sunday is always coming. I receive dozens, even hundreds of e-mails, texts, and phone calls every day.

I know, to be effective, I must make the best use of my time. Plus, I may not be the best person to meet with everyone. Part of my job includes investing time in the staff. And I have to reserve ample time for Bible study, prayer, and sermon preparation. Sometimes I need to refer people to someone who is more available at the time. Some weeks, to be honest, I end up saying no more than yes. My fellow strugglers who want to please everyone will understand this is hard to do, but I must.

If time were limitless, I would always be available. As with most leaders, it is easier for me to say yes than it is to say no. I am always more popular when I do. But popularity is never an effective goal.

Yet here is the other side of not being available: this should not mean I am unreachable, especially to those people I am trying to lead. I genuinely want people to be served and to serve people, so I try to always be accessible.

I hold responsiveness as a huge personal value and lead the team to do likewise. I can easily be found online. I do not hide my basic contact information. I respond to all e-mails and return phone calls within a reasonable time, hopefully by the end of each business day. I always try to help people get the answer they need.

I realize even this does not make everyone happy. Some want me always available—to them. But the goal of leadership is not to make everyone happy; it is to lead people to a better reality than today. To do this, I must make effective use of my time. I must be a better time manager.

I know so many pastors facing burnout. They struggle with effectiveness. Their family life is suffering. All because they have tried to always be available when all they needed was to be accessible. (The church leaders in Acts 6 understood this tension. Read that chapter to see how they addressed it.)

One of the reasons leaders struggle so much with time management is they have a hard time saying no to seemingly good things. There is always another good opportunity available to us. So we commit to things we know we do not have time to do, and either we never do them (which is bad for our reputation), we do not do them well (which is bad for our organization), or we take on so much we become emotionally, physically, and spiritually empty (which is bad for our family and us).

Years ago I decided I would almost always rather hear "no" than "I don't know." Now I love it when a leader admits they do not know something. I believe all leaders have something to learn and should learn first from their teams. But I have a strong objection to hearing "I don't know" when the real answer has already been decided or the best answer is "no." A coward says "I don't know" when they already know their answer is no. A future burned-out leader says "maybe" or "I'll do my best" when they know they will never find the time to do it.

When you know the answer is no, say no.

Weak leaders use phrases like:

- "Let me think about it," which really means I am too scared right now to let you know how I really feel.
- "We might consider this," which really means we will never ever consider this, but I feel better putting you off than looking you in the face with the real answer.
- "Let me pray about it," which really means I have no intention of praying about this, but I sound so much more spiritual when I say I will.
- "We'll see," which really means I have already seen and the future does not look promising for your idea.
- "It could be an option down the road," which really means it will be so far down the road, neither of us will even be here.

Afraid of potential conflict or unpopularity, weak leaders make you believe there is a chance for your idea when they have already decided there is no chance.

What is the damage of saying *maybe* when the real answer is *no*?

Unanswered questions often bring confusion to the team. Energy is wasted on dreaming about something that will never happen. Disappointment is bigger when the person learns the real answer or never receives one. The team loses confidence in the leader. Someone else is often denied an opportunity to do something because a leader committed to doing something that did not need doing.

Strong leaders, even though they know no is not what people want to hear, tell the truth up front. They eliminate the guesswork.

Age and maturity has helped me to discern what I can do and should do based on my strengths, weaknesses, passions, and dreams. It is freeing when we become more certain in who God has wired us to be and who he has not.

Still, I have learned through many different seasons that there are often more opportunities than time in life, even God-honoring, seemingly good opportunities. As I was writing this book, I had to say no to some great opportunities. These were things I would have clearly thought had to be "God appointed." They were things I wanted to do. But as much as they lined up with my strengths, passions, and dreams, I knew I needed to say no to them.

How do you know when to say no to what looks like a good thing, perhaps initially even like a "God thing"? The following are four ways I know when to respond with no.

1. *God's calling on my life says no.*

This trumps all the others. This applies to many decisions, but let me use my vocation as an example. I do not believe I am called to a place as much as I am called to a person, namely, the person of Jesus Christ. I believe God often gives tremendous latitude in where we serve him. There are seasons of life, however, where I know he has positioned me in a place for such a time as this. There are things he has called me to complete in this season of my life. God always has the right to change my assignment, but when he has made the assignment clear, the decisions of yes and no become easy.

2. *My heart does not line up with this decision.*

If I get no peace about saying yes, it is time to wait or say no. This requires consistent prayer and wrestling, but the more I pray, the more confident I am in sensing God's specific will for my life and in this decision. This is how I discerned the no answer to the opportunities I mentioned above.

3. *When it distracts from what God has called me to do.*

I cannot do everything or be everywhere. I can only do what I can do. There is nothing wrong with taking assignments just because I want to do them. If, however, they are going to get in the way of my ultimate calling, the right answer—the often difficult but brave answer—is to say no.

A couple of times I have been given opportunities to do a side part-time job for our denomination or another Christian ministry. It is always something that would fit well with my strengths and interests. It is something I would enjoy doing. But leading a large, established church, plus the speaking and writing commitments I already have, take all the energy I have to give. Understanding this does not take away the interest I may have in the position, but it makes saying no easier.

4. *When my personal strengths and interests do not match the opportunity and I don't sense an urgency from God.*

I have learned situational or physical limitations are not a factor if God is in the mix. He can part waters if they are in the way, so I can do things outside of my strengths. But

God seems to work within my experiences and the gifting he has granted me. Why would he waste the investments he has already made in me? Therefore, apart from a sense God is challenging me in a direction outside my gifting, I can rest within the place where he has been preparing me and say no to those he has not.

This is why, for example, I do not do as much counseling as others do. I do some, but it simply does not fuel me, and so I do not feel I do it well. Others on the team are amazingly gifted in this area, and it gives them energy to counsel people.

Discerning the heart of a decision is critical and requires a consistent, close seeking of the heart of God. I realize it is much easier to write about time management—especially about saying no—than to live it, but learning to effectively use time is critical to surviving as a leader long term.

EFFICIENCY MANAGEMENT

Efficiency management is making sure the organization is structured in a way that best allows healthy growth to occur. The biggest part of this, in my experience, is determining where structure gets in the way.

When I owned a small manufacturing company, I had to learn the language of the industry. I obviously knew the term *bottleneck*, but I never really understood it until it became the difference in my being profitable or not. When the bottom line depends on productivity being at its highest, you learn what the term means firsthand.

A bottleneck is defined as "a point of congestion in a system that occurs when workloads arrive at a given point more quickly than that point can handle them."[5] In an organization, the bottleneck is many times the leader. When this happens, progress stalls, growth is limited, and people are frustrated.

The following are seven characteristics of bottleneck leaders.

1. *Every decision ultimately goes through the leader.* People are annoyed because they feel devalued; their ability to make a good decision is in question. When everyone has to wait for the leader to make a decision, things become awkward and valuable time is wasted. Productivity slows and frustration rises.

2. *New ideas or opinions are discouraged.* People want to be a part of something bigger than themselves, and they want to play a part in helping that something become a reality. When they feel their input is not welcome, they feel stifled, unfulfilled, and unnecessary.

3. *The leader is resistant to change.* I know I just typed this sentence, but I am not even sure I believe those two can go together. Leadership, by definition, involves change. Leaders are taking people somewhere new. You cannot get to something new without implementing change along the way. Part of efficiency management is a leader's being unafraid of change on the team.

4. *There is no clear vision, or information is not readily available.* People flounder because they do not know what to do next. They do not know how things are going or what is important to the leader. This bottleneck encourages laziness in some and discouragement in others.

Leaders who spur movement in an organization are quick with information. They are transparent and continually sharing what they see as the future, that is, as far as they can see.

5. *The leader never delegates.* We will talk about delegation shortly, but when people feel empowered, they think like owners. When the leader takes on unnecessary assignments, the leader is overburdened and the team is underutilized. Both suffer in the long term.

6. *Potential leaders are not recruited but controlled.* Leaders are built through a recruit, invest, and release process. Consider Jesus. He recruited the disciples, invested in them, and then sent them out to do the work. When people are controlled, they never develop, and they learn to resent the leader. (See Myth 7 on controlling leadership later in the book.)

7. *Only the leader can launch a new initiative.* The best leaders I know encourage people to take risks. They create a "go for it" environment. When only the leader is allowed to pull the trigger, the organization faces a huge opportunity cost.

Efficiency management is a critical component of a leader's responsibility as well as the health and growth of an organization.

STRUCTURAL MANAGEMENT

This is the truest form of management, the one I tend to know best as what managers do. This is where rules are written and policies are created. This tells an organization how things are to be done. Good structural management is written to empower more than control. If we are not careful, however, structural management can quickly become micromanagement.

There are times leaders may need to micromanage, such as the following.

When a team member is new to the organization.

New people need to learn the culture and the way things are done. They do not know unless they are told. This does not mean we do not allow them to invent, dream, and discover. But they also need to know how decisions are made, the unwritten rules of the organization, and the internal workings of the environment. It will serve everyone well, and they will be more likely to last longer on the team if these knowns and unknowns are learned early in their tenure.

When a team or team leader has been severely crippled by injury or stress.

A few times in my experience, a team member was not mentally or emotionally capable of making right decisions. It could be something in their personal life or the stress of their work, but I have had to step in and help them more than I normally would. They needed a more structured environment for a season to help them succeed.

When in a state of uncertainty, transition, or change.

I once had a strong leader on the team abruptly quit his position. His team was devastated. I realized the team had relied too much on his leadership and were now lost without him. It required more of my management initially before we could raise up new leadership and better empower everyone on the team.

When tackling a new objective critical to the organization.

This is especially true when, as the senior leader, I am the architect of an idea. The team needs more of my management to make sure things are going the way I envision them. This does not mean the outcome will look exactly like I planned, but the team can waste time and resources trying to figure me out without my input rather than doing productive work. (See the mistake I made in the opening story of chapter 2.)

When a team member is underperforming in relation to others.

As a leader, I feel it is part of my role to help people perform at their highest possible level. Sometimes this requires coaching, sometimes instruction, and sometimes discipline. Part of being a leader is recognizing the potential in people and helping them to realize it within the organization. For a season, to help someone get on track for success on the team (or to discover they are not a fit for the team), I have to manage more closely than I normally prefer.

ADMINISTRATIVE MANAGEMENT

Administration includes security, building maintenance, personnel issues, and budgeting and finance. The size of the organization will determine how much a leader is involved in this part of management, but especially for senior leaders, there should be a general awareness of this form of management.

For example, good leaders know how to keep the organization and its people and assets secure without jeopardizing growth or development. In the retail world a huge part of our job was making sure people did not steal from the company. In 2014 the National Trade Federation said shoplifting, employee theft, and supplier fraud cost the American consumer $44 billion. Limiting loss without running off customers with burdensome demands is a key part of administrative management in a retail environment.

Most of us have exited a store after a purchase and triggered an alarm. Lights flash. People stare. You (or whoever it happens to) are embarrassed. How did this happen? Usually, the cashier failed to remove a security tag from an item. It was an innocent mistake. No one is hurt. You simply return to the counter, the cashier removes the tag, and you are on your way again. No harm, no foul.

But for a split second, you are embarrassed when it happens to you. It feels as though people are thinking something about you that is not true. "You stole something." And yet you did not. "You're an idiot." And yet you are not.

Those alarms place us on the defensive. Even though you did nothing wrong, you feel like everyone thinks you did.

Of course, sometimes people steal things, which is why the theft-detection system exists in the first place. But for you, because of an honest mistake, it's a nuisance.

Cheryl and I saw this happen at a T.J.Maxx store. Yet

instead of obnoxious piercing noises and flashing lights, we heard a polite, easy-to-understand recording:

> Excuse me, but we must have forgotten to remove a security tag from one of the items you purchased. Please return to the cashier's desk and we will be happy to assist you.

I loved it! The customer simply returned to the counter. She was surprised but unalarmed. People seemed to laugh about it. No one was looking for a criminal. Instead, they saw an honest mistake—the store's mistake.

It seemed to communicate: "We are not assuming you did something wrong. We simply want to correct our error."

Genius! Someone at T.J.Maxx thought about how to better lead their administrative management.

Most customers who trigger those alarms are not criminals. They are innocent people. T.J.Maxx is obviously thinking about their paying customers. This is a relationship they want to keep and protect.

It was a great reminder to me of something I say to the team and myself frequently: the way you approach an issue of concern often determines how it is received.

PRODUCTION MANAGEMENT

Production management is the action part of leadership where things get done. Obviously we cannot function long as an organization without being productive. Yet how many churches do you know who talk about missions but never do missions? How many churches preach the value of evangelism, but no one ever shares their faith? How many people value mentoring and discipleship, but they show little progress toward it?

Please let me be candid here: production management is accomplished through delegation. And delegation may be one of the hardest things for many leaders to do. There are three primary reasons a leader does not delegate.

1. *Fear.* They are afraid someone else will mess it up or they will look bad for not doing it themselves.
2. *Pride.* They do not believe anyone else can do it, or they believe it will not be done well if they do not do it themselves.
3. *Ignorance.* They have simply never learned the power of delegation—how it impacts progress and how it develops people.

Yet an organization cannot grow until a leader learns to delegate.

I encounter many leaders who claim to want delegation to be part of their leadership. They know its value, but they are often frustrated with the results they receive on delegated projects. So they tend to control the project (which is not delegation) or do everything themselves.

Often I hear both sides as to why delegation fails. A leader may feel they have done their job simply by delegating. The blame naturally shifts to the delegate, who should have figured out how to do the work. The delegate, however, feels overwhelmed, like they did not have the freedom, resources, or knowledge to complete the project to the leader's expectations. Both sides are frustrated. Many times the problem rests with the way the project was delegated from the beginning. There are certainly times when the delegate drops the ball and does not follow through with the task. But in my experience, the failure of delegation most often rests with the leader.

The following are five reasons delegation fails.

1. *A predetermined win was never clear or understood.*

Everyone needs to be on the same page as to what should be accomplished. Furthermore, there should be accountability in place prior to delegation. When someone receives a project, they need to be given a timeline for completion. They need a system of follow-up, measures of accomplishment, and benchmarks toward completion.

2. *The leader dumped or controlled instead of delegated.*

In healthy delegation, the leader retains a level of responsibility to check in periodically with the delegate's progress. At the same time, it is delegation. There is a release of direct oversight that needs to take place. The delegate should feel they have the freedom to accomplish the predetermined objective in their own way. There is a balance and partnership in a healthy delegation process, where the leader remains close enough to assure completion but distant enough to let people do their work.

3. *The delegate was not properly prepared.*

Assuming someone knows how to do a task and can figure out a way on their own is not only naive but unfair. Questions need to be asked and information given at the front end to make sure the delegate has the ability to complete the task or the ability to learn along the way. This may involve the leader's spending more time in the beginning phases of a task to ensure completion is attainable by the delegate. Specialized training may be needed. In fact, a failed delegation may be just the experience someone needs to do a better job next time.

4. *Adequate resources were not in place.*

It is difficult to expect someone to complete a task when the leader has not given them the proper tools for the job. Sometimes anxious leaders delegate a project too soon, before the team is ready, either in structure, people power, or resources.

5. *The wrong person was chosen for the task.*

Let's face it, not everyone is up to every task. Many times delegation fails because the leader picked the wrong person for the job. Selecting the best person on the front end or reassigning the task when an improper fit is discovered is critical to assure completion of a task.

If these are reasons why delegation fails, how can we do delegation effectively? The following are the five necessary ingredients for healthy delegation.

1. *Expectations*

The delegate needs to know the goals and objectives the leader wants to achieve. They need to know what a win looks like in the leader's mind. The clearer the leader can make this, the more successful the delegation will be. Most people want to please their leader. Everyone wants to know they did good work. The questions "Why are we doing this?" and "What are we trying to accomplish?" should be answered distinctly in their mind.

2. *Knowledge*

The leader should be sure the proper training, coaching, and education have been received. The leader should remain available during the process so questions or uncertainties of details that arise can be answered.

3. *Resources*

Good delegation involves having adequate resources and money to accomplish the assigned task. Nothing is more frustrating than being asked to complete a project without the tools with which to do it.

4. *Accountability*

Proper delegation involves follow-up and evaluation of the assignment. This is healthy for the leader, the delegate, and the organization.

5. *Appreciation*

Delegation is not complete until the leader recognizes the delegate's accomplishment. Failing to do so limits the leader's ability to continue healthy delegation in the future. No one wants to assist an ungrateful leader.

PEOPLE MANAGEMENT

Perhaps the most important form of management in a leader's job is people management. This is the process of helping people do their work, feel like a part of the team, and participate in professional development. This subject probably deserves its own chapter, but I will share some attributes leaders should have for good people management.

Awareness

Good leaders know their team. We talked about this in an earlier chapter, but people are individuals. They have unique expectations and require different things from leadership. Some require more attention and some less. Whether through personality profiles or just getting to know them over time, leaders should learn about the people they are supposed to be leading.

Openness

Good leaders let their team know them as a person outside of the role as leader. They are transparent enough so the team can learn to trust the leader.

Responsiveness

Good leaders do not leave people waiting too long for a response. People will make up their own responses if the leader does not respond—and it is usually not the conclusion the leader wants them to reach.

Approachable

A leader cannot be everything to everyone and may not always be available, but for the team they are called to lead or manage, they need to be approachable. They need to know if there is a problem or a concern. A leader will be receptive to hearing from their team. The larger the organization, the more difficult this is, so we need to build systems that allow us to hear from people at every level within the organization.

Consistency

Over time the team needs to learn a leader is dependable. The world is changing fast. It is hard to know who to trust. We certainly need to be able to trust the people we are supposed to follow.

Trustworthy

A leader needs to follow through on what they say they will do. If a leader makes a promise, they should keep it. If they cannot support something, they should say it. If they are not going to do something, they should say no. A leader's word should be their bond. Good leaders spend time building and protecting their character. They are the quality of person they would want to follow.

Appreciative

Good leaders recognize they cannot achieve any level of success alone. They are grateful, rewarding, and celebratory.

They love others and want to serve them, and they display it genuinely in tangible ways.

People management is hard, and it is the weakest area for many leaders. The problem for many leaders is they do not really want to lead. They just want people to follow.

My friend Bob is a visionary pastor and leader. He walks into a room and people are ready to follow him. I have often wished I had his charisma. God has used Bob in some incredible ways. He has learned over the years, however, he is a terrible manager. He simply cannot effectively manage an organization. The only way he knows to lead people is to tell them what to do. As a result, he hires lots of people who are eager to work with him, but he does not keep them very long. In fact, in Bob's current church, other leaders recognize this in Bob and basically took the management of the church away from him. He casts a vision for the church, but someone else manages it.

Sadly, many people assume leadership and management are equal functions. We want environments where team members are free to create, but every team also needs some guidelines and someone who can hold the team accountable to some reasonable boundaries it sets for itself. Management's role in implementing a vision is to ensure that tasks and action steps are met. Good management helps the team stay on target. While leadership motivates the team to reach the vision, a team without management will have a lot of dreams but no measurable results. Managers help to develop and maintain a structure that allows healthy growth to continue.

Do not be afraid of good management. Great organizations need both management and leadership, but they are not equal and they require different skills. If you are a leader, part of your role is to ensure healthy management is in place. If you are not reaching the goals you have for the organization, it may not be for a lack of good leadership; it may be a lack of good management. For smaller teams, one person may have the responsibility for both functions, which is hard for many wired more toward being a leader or a manager type, but great organizations need both good leadership and good management.

 MYTH 5

Being the Leader Makes Me Popular

I HAD A COUPLE OF SPEAKING ENGAGEMENTS IN Nashville. We are from the area and have a son and daughter-in-law who still live there, so Cheryl always goes with me when I am going to be in town. One day was an especially good day. We had seen our son in the morning before he left town on business. I spoke to what appeared to be an attentive audience, receiving lots of praise for my talks. We had a nice, leisurely afternoon at the hotel. It was a beautiful spring day, and I sat out by the pool to read and write. Glorious!

Nashville has some trendy coffee shops, so in the evening, Cheryl wanted to go to one she had been to earlier in the week. I pulled into the parking lot; it was packed but we found an open spot in front of a business next door that was closed for the day. We were going to buy something to go but then chose to sit for a minute and enjoy our coffee. We were probably in the shop about fifteen minutes.

When we walked to the parking lot, the strangest feeling occurred. Where did we park? Have you ever forgotten where you parked your car? Well, it would not be unusual for me, but it was highly unusual for Cheryl. It took us a few minutes to realize we had not forgotten where we parked. Our car was simply not where we left it.

Then I noticed the sign: "PARKING FOR BUSINESS ONLY. VIOLATORS WILL BE TOWED AT THE OWNER'S EXPENSE." And it listed a number to call. Now we knew why we could not find our car. We had parked in a neighboring business parking lot, which was closed for the evening, along with dozens of other cars—but ours was the out-of-town license plate.

Long story and $135 later—it would have been another $50 if we were more than two hours in paying the fine to get our car—we had our car back and went on with our evening a little less peppy than before. Frustrating! I learned a lot from the experience, such as that towing signs should be taken seriously and the whole towing thing may be a racket. (I am not bitter or anything.)

It was also a tremendous leadership reminder.

One moment you may be the most powerful and popular person in the room. Everyone loves you. It is the best day ever. And the next moment you are not! And the day stinks.

One minute you are the hot speaker in town for the day, celebrating at a trendy coffee shop. The next minute you are the guy scrambling to find enough cash to get your car out of a fenced lot guarded by angry dogs who do not wag their tails, from an unsmiling man who's behind a window, smoking, wearing a too-small, stained white T-shirt, and does not take kindly to those who joke about inconvenience and the cost of reclaiming a car. (I am not bitter or anything.)

Everything can change in a single minute.

One minute you are enjoying your team in a staff meeting, the team is working well together, ideas are flowing, everyone is excited about what is happening around them—and the next minute a key associate tells you they are resigning.

One minute you are celebrating a successful season in sales—and the next minute you lose one of your best customers.

One minute you are celebrating the church's phenomenal last quarter—and the next minute you are bombarded by someone with a dozen complaints they have been saving for the seemingly right opportunity to unload on you.

One minute everyone thinks you are wonderful and cannot brag on you enough—and the next minute it seems like you have a "kick me" sign on your back.

These days usually are Mondays for a pastor. A pastor's worst day is often the day after a great Sunday. I love whoever said they do not take off Mondays, because why would they want to be miserable on their day off?

Oh, the woes of leadership.

We often believe being the leader makes you popular. Wrong! This is what it could mean on *some* days and in *some* circles. But it could also mean you are the target of everyone's frustration.

Here is what I have learned in leadership. Learn this and it will be worth the cost of this book. To be successful long term as a leader, you have to learn to navigate the highs and lows of leadership.

Over the years, I have had staff members who wanted to sit where I sit but not necessarily experience what I experience. If you want to be a leader, you have to be able to withstand the heat in the kitchen.

JIM'S STORY

Jim, a senior pastor, and I worked together on a leadership issue that was causing harm to the church. Jim wanted me to help him think through how best to address the issue. It was a personnel issue, which are always the hardest.

One of the staff members (let's call him Kirk) was considered a lousy team player by the rest of the staff. He was lazy, divisive, and disrespectful to Jim. He really did not add much value to the team, mostly because he had checked out years earlier. Kirk was not happy, but he was too comfortable in his position (and with his pay) to go somewhere else.

Based on what you know so far, this seems like an easy decision to make. But maybe this is my former business background talking. If I simply encouraged Jim to do the right thing, it would be to advise him that the wayward staff member needs to go because of the flippancy he was showing toward his work and the leadership team.

But life and leadership are seldom this easy.

You can almost see it coming. Kirk was extremely popular with the people in the church. They loved him. They loved his family. They had watched his children grow up, and now the children were also popular in the church. There was hardly a family not connected to Kirk's family in some way. On

Sundays and Wednesdays there was not a better known or more respected staff member.

Jim was in a tough spot. (Churches notoriously struggle with this type of personnel issue.)

The problem was, there are seven days in a week, not just the two where everyone loved Kirk.

Jim and other key leaders in the church knew that something needed to change. Kirk had been counseled and threatened with losing his job numerous times over the years, but he knew he was popular. He knew there could be huge ramifications by dismissing him, and so he refused to change. Kirk was, according to Jim, even arrogant about his job security at times.

Jim had not been at the church as long as Kirk had, and he was still trying to gain the trust of the church. Jim was popular—still in a honeymoon period—but he felt he might never recover if he fired Kirk.

This is a reminder of another important leadership principle: making a decision is often easy, but the right solution can often be hard to find.

I saw three options on the table. One, Jim could fire Kirk and live with the consequences. He might not be as popular, but he would have eliminated a problem. Two, Jim could leave. Life is short. Go find another pastorate. Since this situation was making his life miserable, he could simply begin again somewhere else. Three, Jim could learn to live with the problem. He remains popular, but the problem is not solved. Perhaps over time he would develop enough trust to do something about the problem.

There. Easy enough, right? I did my job by providing a

clear path for a decision. Jim simply had to choose the one that seemed best to him. Make a decision. He could even draw numbers out of a hat if he could not decide. (One for fire, two for quit, and three for live with it.)

But, again, finding the solution to a problem is much more difficult than picking numbers out of a hat. Answers may appear easy, but finding a solution is a wrenching process.

Finding solutions involves hard decisions and dealing with hard consequences. In this case, the solution could be any of the three easy answers. But sometimes a solution is bigger than making a decision. To be a solution, it involves follow-through, cleanup, and working through a situation for the ultimate good of the church. This is the hard, messy, difficult work of leadership. Sometimes we hope there will be some easy answer if we talk to enough people, which is part of the solution. But this is seldom the case.

And Jim's popularity as a leader was on the line as well.

He really had only three options, in my opinion. Oh, there are tons of scenarios within each, but ultimately it would come down to one of these three. And I did not feel I could make the decision for Jim. Since he would have to live with the consequences, the decision would have to be his.

I think Jim already knew what he had to do. The question was, would he make a decision (and doing nothing is making a decision) or would he solve the problem? Regardless of the risk to his popularity, would he do the right thing?

Great leaders do not simply make decisions; they find solutions. They find the best solutions for the vision and the organization in spite of how unpopular it makes them. And many times, doing the right thing has a negative impact on popularity—at least in the short term.

I call it the loneliness of leadership.

Tom, another friend,[1] and I were talking about some difficult decisions he faced for his organization regarding payroll costs. He has too many people on staff for the volume of work. The industry has changed, and it is not likely to change for the good. He may never need as many people again. He knows what is right and necessary simply to continue to survive as a company, but he also knows the decision will be very unpopular with those who lose their jobs and with those who will stay on as employees. Since this is a family business, Tom will most likely lose long-term friendships as a result of the decisions he has to make.

I sympathized with Tom, because I have led a small business. We should have made harder decisions than we made at times.

But I reminded Tom of something all leaders need to know. There is sometimes a loneliness in leadership that cannot be avoided. And we should not offer to lead if we are not willing to sometimes stand alone.

Even in the best team environments, there will be times when the direction the organization needs to go involves decisions that adversely affect the team. Consider, for example, some of the hard decisions the manufacturing industries in the United States have been forced to make in order to remain viable. With ever-evolving technology, there simply are not as many manufacturing jobs as there once were. And this is true even for companies that would never farm out work to other countries. The companies that survive may be the ones willing to make the hardest choices.

There have been times when I have to have hard conversations to correct people who are wrong or follow through on a plan I believe in my gut is best for the church or organization—even though it is unpopular—all because I happen to sit in the leader's chair. The responsibility of a leader should never be abused as an excuse for dictatorship or poor leadership, but loneliness sometimes comes with being a leader.

Our youngest son, Nathaniel, preached for me once. As we left the church—I am usually one of the last ones there—I was turning out the lights in the hallways and classrooms. I did not realize it, but I must have mumbled about it. "I wish these people would turn out the lights. It drives me crazy how they leave every light on in this building. What is so hard about turning them off?" I probably grumbled a lot about the lights. There are a lot of lights.

Nathaniel, at the time a youth pastor at another church, said, "Pops (he started calling me Pops when he was in high school), let me help you with something."

"Okay, son. Help me." (I love when our children get old enough to supposedly help us.)

"When the senior leader has this one pet peeve about something, it says to the other staff members they don't see any of the other things we are doing right. Like that's all you care about."

Good insight. But I responded, "I appreciate this good piece of information. And I agree with you. But let me help you with something. First, I don't have just one pet peeve. I have many pet peeves. More important, when I came here, we were hundreds of thousands of dollars in the hole. We have gradually been finding our way out of that financial mess. But, you see, our electric bill runs somewhere around half a million dollars a year. And we are terrible about wasting electricity. If we could save just ten percent on our electric bill, we could add fifty thousand dollars to the student ministry budget."

Nathaniel helped me turn off the rest of the lights.

There are times I have to be the proverbial bad guy about an issue if it is for the betterment of the entire church. Ultimately, turning off lights has a kingdom purpose, because it is being a wise steward of the finances with which God has entrusted us. There are some things I simply have to enforce as a leader. It does not necessarily make me popular though.

Having been a senior leader in business, government, and the church, I would say that leading can be more challenging in the church. There are more bosses for the pastor, certainly more who feel they have entitled opinions. This may be one of the leading causes of pastor burnout and why so many never finish their vocational careers as pastors.

Pastoring—and leadership—can be lonely.

Granted, as a pastor I am supposed to find my strength in Christ. (You have to know how helpful it is to be reminded of that whenever I express a sense of stress, and it is usually said as if pastors are commanded to rely on Christ and others are not.) I do seek Christ as my ultimate strength. I teach the Bible as truth and I know the Scriptures, but the Bible also says we should be "bearing with one another in love" (Eph. 4:2). God did not design us to do life alone. This goes for pastors too.

From my experience, those in ministry leadership are some of the loneliest people. I hear from them every day.

While I was talking with a young pastor recently, he said, "Who is going to invest in me?" Good question.

I understand the sentiment. He is struggling for answers he cannot seem to find. Practical answers. People are looking to him for leadership, but seminary did not teach him all he needs to know. I think every good leader needs to ask this question—hopefully often.

Later that week, I was talking to an older pastor. He said, "I go home most days and haven't heard a single positive word. Things are going great. We are growing faster than ever, but it seems I get far more of the negatives than I get to hear of the good we are doing."

All I could do was agree. I have felt like this many times.

HOW TO SURVIVE

When the heavy weight of ministry or leadership responsibility appears to rest on your shoulders, when everyone looks to you for the answers, when some days you do not know which direction to turn, when you are balancing the demands of ministry and family, when you are seen as a key in helping everyone with a problem hold their life together, yet you feel no one is concerned about your personal struggles and you do not know who to trust . . . welcome to the ministry!

Of course, this impacts all leaders, not simply pastors. But what do you do during seasons of ministry and seasons of life when all of this lands on your shoulders?

Yes, you start by remembering God's words of encouragement, such as "Casting all your care upon Him, for He cares for you" (1 Peter 5:7). This is the first answer.

But never believe it is wrong if this is not enough, like somehow you are less spiritual because you need others. You do. I do. All God's children should say "Amen!"

So, next, I suggest you find a mentor. Find someone who is walking farther down the road from you but going in the direction you want to go.

A word to pastors here: do not think your mentor has to be another pastor. It could be, but it may be someone in the business world who loves Jesus and has more experience in life and leadership than you. Some of my best mentors have been leading businesspeople—some attended our church and some did not. And some of my mentors have been pastors. The point is, do not limit yourself to the title.

Also, regularly surround yourself with a few pastors or leaders at the same level you are organizationally. (Senior leader, middle manager, entry level, etc.) It seems to work best if the organizations are similar in size and structure. Those leaders will best understand your context.

Work to develop a close enough relationship with them over time, where you can trust them. You may have to spend some of your free time and even travel to do this. Learn from each other, seek wisdom from each other, and grow together in the ministry.

Again, a word to pastors: these people do not necessarily have to be in vocational ministry. In one of the most helpful peer leadership groups I have been a part of, I was the only pastor. I believe in connecting with the community, so the other people included a police chief, a school director, and a newspaper publisher. We all had in common trying to lead people and feeling the pressure at times in attempting to do so.

Regardless of the makeup of your group, the point is to consistently share your burdens, concerns, and encouragements with one another. You can do this in person occasionally but more frequently over the phone or online. Chances are they need this as much as you do, so be the one to take the initiative.

You may be thinking those groups are not there for you. You have tried before and could not find them. Many pastors and leaders have burned out before trying to find people to invest in them. To this, I say keep trying. It is worth it. Treat this like any other friendship. It takes commitment and has to be a balance of give and take. Be willing to be vulnerable. Risk rejection to extend an offer for friendship. Use social media, denominational leadership, and recommendations from others to find these pastors or leaders. Do whatever is necessary. (This, by the way, has been one of the greatest benefits of social media for me.)

I have had to develop some of these relationships outside my city. I have found they are valuable enough to justify the time and financial investment required.

The key? It takes intentional effort. If you see the value, be willing to make the commitment required to find the right people—whether a mentor or a peer group—to keep you strong and help make you a better leader. Bill Hybels observed, "Everyone wins when a leader gets better."[2] But it takes intentionality to make it happen. I have never had a mentor or a peer group where I was not directly involved in bringing the relationship together. But I have also never had one that did not improve me in some way, whether in leadership or in my personal life. And both of those have been beneficial to me personally as well as the organization I was trying to lead.

In leadership, it's important to recognize the difference between popularity and trust. Many leaders confuse the two. Many assume they are trusted because they are popular, but many times this is not the case. You may be extremely popular. Everyone may love you personally. But it doesn't mean they trust you. Popularity does not always equal trust.

I have seen leaders—pastors, politicians, businesspeople— try to take people places, even worthy places, and believe they would follow because they are popular leaders. But people did not follow, because the leader had not developed enough trust. Misunderstanding this can dramatically damage a leader's performance, especially newer leaders.

Popularity has some importance in leadership. It is easier to follow a leader we like personally. But popularity may be seasonal and temporary. Popularity can be altered by successes and disappointments. Popularity can cause followers to cheer or jeer, because whether it is good or bad, popularity is mostly built on emotion.

If this reality were not true, my file of criticism would be so much smaller. In reality, in some seasons, it is larger than my encouragement file. The only way to avoid criticism and always be popular as a leader is to make no decisions, do nothing different, never challenge the status quo—in other words, do nothing.

Trust is needed at the biggest moments in leadership. Major changes involve trust. Times of uncertainty need established trust in leadership. Long-term success requires trust. And trust must be earned.

Trust develops with time and experience. Trust invokes a deeper level of loyalty and commitment, which helps people weather the storms of life together. Trust develops roots in a relationship that grow far deeper than popularity can.

The problem for us as leaders is that popularity often disguises itself as trust when people appear to be agreeing with you. It may fool you into thinking you can do anything, because you are, after all, popular. But here is the thing: if you proceed with the false assumption that popularity is trust, wait until you cross the wrong line of people's level of trust and you will see a backlash against your leadership. Suddenly you did or said the wrong thing, and now no one wants to follow you anymore. They did not trust you, and now you are not even popular.

You will be a more effective leader when you begin to discern when you are popular (which feels so good for a while) and when you are trusted. Trust takes longer and is harder to develop, but the good feelings that come with it last for a lifetime.

A SOBERING LEADERSHIP REALITY

Here is another hard word for pastors who live to be popular. This is a sobering reality every leader needs to understand:

the longer you do what you do well, the less praise you will receive for it.

If you do not understand this principle, you will often feel disappointed. You'll feel that no one cares, that they do not even notice the good work you are doing, that you are no longer popular.

The fact is that everyone loves to praise the new guy (guest appearances, surprise home runs). One of my favorite examples is the Sunday guest speaker who has delivered the same message forty-two times before and has gotten really good at it. Everyone calls it the best sermon ever. But when you have been there awhile, trying to do well every week, and you hit a home run more times than the average speaker, the cheers may not be as loud.

Once you have been exceptional for a while, that becomes the new norm. It is expected. It is now your new average. Everyone expects you to be wonderful all the time. They have gained a certain confidence in your ability. Thus, you can naturally expect to hear less approval. You will hear fewer "good jobs" and fewer "you were amazing" comments. That doesn't mean you aren't doing a good job anymore. Nor does it mean you aren't popular anymore. It just means you have set the bar of expectation a little higher for yourself.

Of course, part of improving is continually raising our own bar of expectations. But if you are realizing this sobering reality, you have done something right long enough to reach a new personal plateau. And for this, I would say, "Congratulations!"

This principle is a warning of sorts. The quietness of the

new norm can make you think you are no longer appreciated, no longer popular. If you are not careful, you will begin to doubt your abilities or the success you are still having. Those emotions—and your reactions to them—are normal, even if they are not true.

I am not ignoring the times when you are not doing your best. Do not be an unaware leader. Redefining normal is part of being a leader. We need to continually get better as leaders.

When you are not feeling very loved or popular, you need to seek your affirmation beyond the verbal praise of others. If you live for the praise of others, you will eventually be controlled by their praise (or lack thereof). I would remind you that you may be doing everything right, but you seldom hear about all the good you are doing. And whether it is right or not, this is understandable. It's part of leadership. The leader who can lead just as passionately toward a noble goal without the praise of others—even perhaps in times when criticism seems more dominant—is on track for success.

The fact is, our goal as leaders should not be popularity. As leaders, we should consider whether we are willing to pay the price for good leadership, willing to sacrifice popularity for progress. It is not easy being a good leader. Every hard decision a leader makes excites some and upsets others.

At the same time, most of us who have positions of leadership want people to like us personally and as their leader. We all want to be liked. This pursuit, however, leads many leaders to becoming victims of people pleasing, wanting people to like us as our first goal. When pleasing people becomes our primary objective, we seldom lead people into what is best and are led more by the opinions of others than by a vision or any determined goals.

PEOPLE-PLEASING

Every leader knows that people-pleasing is not a good quality for a leader. But after talking with hundreds of pastors every year, I have to say this has to be one of the greatest weaknesses they confess to me. When pastors aim to please people, they are motivated more by what people want than by what God wants for the church. This is obviously dangerous. Hopefully, I do not have to build a case here.

What are the casualties of people-pleasing? What are the organizational casualties? How does it ultimately play out among the people in the church or the organization we are attempting to lead? Knowing these answers may help us be more determined not to allow people-pleasing to be our motivation in our leadership. The following are six casualties of people-pleasers.

1. *No one is ever really satisfied.*

When the leader tries to please everyone, the reality is that no one on the team finds fulfillment in their work. No one. In an attempt to let everyone win, no one really does. The people we are trying to lead are only as happy as when we are making decisions the way they would want us to make them.

My best sermon in people's minds is the one in which I address a current need in their lives or I am challenging someone else's sin. I could preach on suffering every week, and someone would say it was my best sermon. I hardly ever hear this, though, when I preach on tithing. I know this by experience, but how biblical would it be for me to preach to be popular?

2. Tension mounts among the team.

As the leader attempts to please everyone, people are pitted against one another. Team members are conditioned to jockey for position with their leaders, aimed at pleasing them. This creates a political atmosphere among people who should be working together.

I know a pastor who appears to tell you what you want to hear when you have a suggestion or a complaint. He does this for everyone, even when there are opposing viewpoints. It does not take long for these to come to light. How do you think people feel when they discover what they were told was not necessarily how the pastor felt? It ultimately leads to disloyalty.

3. Disloyalty is rampant.

You might think that people-pleasing should build loyal supporters, but actually the reverse is true. Since the people-pleaser says what people want to hear more than what needs to be said, people subsequently do not trust the people-pleaser. They quickly learn what the leader says is not the whole truth but rather what will keep the leader popular.

4. Burnout is common.

I have observed team members trying to function under a people-pleaser. They feel they have the leader's support, but then it is pulled out from under them as the leader tries to please someone else. It is tiring, frustrating, and wrong. People-pleasing leads to teams being fractured as well as the vision toward which they were working.

5. *Mediocrity reigns.*

Second best becomes the standard under a people-pleasing leader, as the leader refuses to push for everyone's best and settles for what will keep the leader popular. Lackluster results ultimately lower standards. In an effort to please everyone, the team compromises what could be wonderful for what keeps the majority of people temporarily happy (emphasis on *temporarily*).

6. *Visions stall.*

Visions are intended to take us places. Noble places we have never been. This involves change. Always. And change is hard. Always. People do not like change. People-pleasers want people to be happy. You see where this is going?

This might be a good place to pause and allow you to evaluate how much of a people-pleaser you are as a leader. We can all be one to some extent. If the scale were one to ten, with ten being the ultimate people-pleaser, what number are you? More important, how much is it damaging the quality of your leadership?

If you feel you are a people-pleaser, you may be wondering what you can do about it. Let me offer a few suggestions:

1. *Get firm again on the vision you are trying to accomplish.*

If people-pleasing is a problem for you, it must be more important to you than accomplishing your vision. Not to sound harsh, but this is simply your reality. We tend to do what we value most. You must begin to value the vision more than making people happy. Make sure it is God honoring and God ordained. When you are leading a church, obviously you want to do the will of God. He gives us latitude, I believe, but we want to make sure whatever we do honors him and gives him glory.

The vision, though, is what should hold your feet to the fire. If it detracts or does not line up with the vision God has given you, you should not be as enthusiastic about it, regardless of who brings it to you. This does not mean you cannot say yes to other things, but you can clearly say, "I am sorry, but right now I am chasing this vision God has given me." Imagine the pressure Moses was under as a leader to please the people, but he had to hold to the vision God had given him and not cave to the pressure to always please people.

2. *Get buy-in with a team toward reaching the vision.*

You need a team around you that is committed to the same defined vision you have. Be careful who you surround yourself with here. Make sure they are people who are not self-serving, can see a bigger picture, and will protect your back should the need arise. You will need others, however, who can back you up when you are tempted to give in and be a people-pleaser.

When you recruit them, make sure they understand the vision and are committed to seeing it to completion. Be honest with your propensity to cave to pressure from others. Share with them your desire to complete the vision and give them permission to speak into your life when they see you pleasing people more than accomplishing the vision.

3. *Assign responsibility and time lines.*

This may seem too mechanical, but it will keep you on track when complaints rise. Give people real responsibility toward accomplishing the vision and measurable time lines toward achievement. This is hard for some leaders, but you have to release responsibility for decisions that need to be made. This process is vital, because it keeps tasks moving forward and makes it easier and more palatable when you have to say no to other things. It is hard to argue with success.

I find it is sometimes easier for someone closer to a task to say no to something new. For example, if a group wants us to start a new mission somewhere outside our focus area, the people currently leading our mission efforts are often better at protecting the vision we have already set in place than I. If I let those who lead in a specific area of ministry help make the decisions in their area, they will protect the vision. I will be less concerned with being popular and more concerned with the vision.

Allow these same people to hold you accountable to stick to these determined goals and objectives. I give people on my team the right to challenge me when I am veering from the vision we share.

4. *Discipline yourself.*

If you recognize that people pleasing is a weakness in your leadership, you will have to discipline yourself away from it. No one else can ultimately do this for you. And it will take time. It probably has been a weakness for a while, so do not expect it to disappear immediately. When you sense you are making a decision purely to please others, check yourself. Tie a string around your finger if need be, but through practice and consistency focus on the bigger picture.

When needed, call in your trusted advisors. Renew your passion for the vision. Slowly, over time, you will find yourself better able to say no so you can realize the vision God has placed on your heart.

HANDLING CRITICISM

Another aspect of the popularity issue concerns criticism. And let's be honest, criticism hurts. No one enjoys hearing something negative about them or finding out something they did was not perceived well by others. One reason we like to be popular as leaders is because we do not like to be criticized.

The fact is, however, criticism accompanies leadership. Every leader needs to know this. Make any decision, and some will agree with you and some will not. The only way to avoid criticism as a leader is to do nothing. If a leader is taking an organization somewhere, and even if they are not, someone will criticize their efforts.

This said, the way a leader responds to criticism creates the culture for receiving feedback in the future. It says a lot about the maturity of the leader and the quality of their leadership. And it should be determined regardless of whether it makes the leader popular.

There are four wrong ways to respond to criticism.

1. *Find fault with the critic.*

Instead of admitting there might be any validity to a criticism, many leaders immediately attempt to discredit the person or the group offering it. Granted, someone may be at fault—some people are terrible complainers. I have also learned that some people are mean. They get buzzed by stirring up controversy and seeing how others respond to it. But it is never helpful to start there.

When we brought needed change to an established church, we received our share of criticism. The reality was that most of the criticism came from people who had been in the church for many years and had grown accustomed to the ways things had always been done. Their tenure usually meant they were also of an older generation. I found myself dreading every time a senior citizen said they wanted to talk to me. I immediately assumed it was a complaint. It was not a fair generalization. Sometimes they simply wanted to bring me some homegrown tomatoes or even homemade desserts. (Those are good days in leadership!)

2. *Blame others.*

In elementary school it went like this, "I know I am, but what are you?" Often a leader will receive criticism, and instead of analyzing whether there is any validity or not, the leader begins to shift the focus toward others by criticizing other organizations or leaders. Even if they realize the criticism may be valid, they are not willing to accept personal responsibility, so they pass it along to others. This is dangerous on so many levels and is truly poor leadership. It is a very immature response.

One of my early leadership mentors was my high school principal. Perhaps the best principle he instilled in me is to take ownership of my actions and not blame others. For example, as student body president, I would get frustrated with people not performing to the expectations I had for them. My principal would challenge me that maybe I was not clear with my expectations. I needed this "ouch."

3. *Ignore an opportunity to learn.*

This is a big one, because criticism can be a great teaching tool. The truth is, there is usually something to be learned from all criticism. It may need a filter, though. The person offering the criticism and their circumstances need to be taken into consideration, but with every criticism comes an opportunity to learn something positive for the organization or about the leader.

In my first church, I would preach, give an invitation, and then pray to close out the service. During my prayer, I would walk toward the back of the platform. When I said "Amen," I was out the door and disappearing to my office. I thought this was an act of humility. It kept people from feeling obligated to compliment the message. The truth is, it was more comfortable for me and my introverted nature.

After a few months of doing this every Sunday, an elderly

deacon told me, "Preacher, when you're saying your prayer at the end of the service, if you'll walk to the front of the church instead of the back, and shake people's hands when they leave, they'll be more likely to come back next week."

I needed to hear this. It was an appropriate challenge. After his suggestion, I have been doing this ever since. As the churches where I pastor have grown larger, I have had to be more creative to shake more hands, but now it is a signature part of our church. People know the pastor wants to know them. And I do. I did before, but I was not acting as if I did.

4. *Appease.*

This last one is huge, and I have seen it so many times. Many leaders are so fearful of conflict that they attempt to satisfy all their critics, even if they never intend to follow through or make any changes because of the criticism. They say what the critic wants to hear. They become the people-pleasers.

The healthy response if there is no merit to criticism is not to act like there is merit. We should be kind, but we should not be accommodating.

I have been guilty of all of these at one time or another. Awareness is half the battle. Identifying the wrong ways to respond to criticism and working to correct them in your leadership is part of growing as a leader.

Criticism, however, is still a part of leadership. It comes with the territory. And if handled correctly, it does not have to be a bad part of leadership, or at least not as bad as we make it out to be. Allowing criticism to work for you and not against you is a key to maturing as a leader.

The following are four right ways to respond to criticism.

1. *Listen to everyone.*

You may not respond to everyone the same way, but everyone deserves a voice and everyone should be treated with respect. As leaders, we need to at least listen to their criticism, especially when people are willing to put their name behind it.

Because I know someone will think about it, this is somewhat different with anonymous criticism. It is hard to give respect to someone you do not know. I am different from some leaders, because I do read anonymous criticism and pay attention to it, especially if it appears valid. I have often learned from anonymous criticism. Plus, I always wonder if something in my leadership prompted the anonymous response. At the same time, I never criticize leaders who do not listen to anonymous criticism. I do not, however, weigh unidentified criticism as heavily as I do criticism from a person willing to own it.

2. *Consider the source.*

One of the most helpful tools for me in leadership has been to use a stakeholder's analysis when dealing with criticism. When I consider a person's interest and power or influence in the organization, it can affect the way I respond in making a decision, determining who's involved in that process, and helping us to stay focused on the mission while still valuing people.

The diagram on the next page demonstrates this.[3]

In a stakeholder sense, how much influence and investment does this person have in the organization? This might not change your answer to the criticism, but it may affect the amount of energy you invest in your answer. If you have an individual on your team with high interest and high power, such as a passionate key leader, you may react differently to their concern over an issue than you would react to a random person in your community.

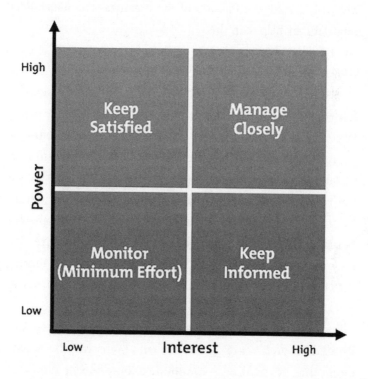

For example, years ago our church met in two schools. If the director of schools had criticism for me, I would invest more time in responding to him than if the criticism came from a one-time visitor who was complaining about our music and told me that she would never return.

I realize some may see this process as cold or even uncaring, but I see it as a paradigm for applying the best wisdom to a circumstance. Ultimately, I think our goal as leaders should be to bring the best voices to the table—even in criticism—and eliminate obstacles involving people who have little real interest in what we're trying to accomplish. We have to value people and still protect the mission of the organization. Stakeholder analysis may help with this.

3. *Analyze for validity.*

After you have considered the source of the criticism, you have to look at the criticism itself. Is it true? This is where maturity as a leader is most important. You have to check your ego, because there is often an element of truth even to criticism with which you do not agree completely. Do not dismiss the criticism until you have considered what is true and what is not. Mature leaders are willing to admit their faults and recognize the areas of needed improvement. Look for common themes. If you receive the same criticism from more than one source, perhaps there is a problem even though you can't see it. You can learn something from any criticism if you are willing to look for trends.

When analyzing for validity, keep in mind this may not be a vision problem or a problem with your strategy or programming. It could be a communication problem. Not long ago a man came to my office to complain about the care he had received while he was hospitalized. He did not feel the staff had adequately visited him or shown him the attention he felt we should have. I listened to him and tried to apologize for the way he felt, but I knew something else was wrong, because our church has a tremendous care system. I asked him a series of questions and discovered there were some problems with the way information flowed between the different ministries of our church. We had a good system in place, but we needed to add something more in our internal communication. We simply never knew he was hospitalized.

4. *Give an answer.*

Criticism is like asking a question. It deserves an answer even if the answer is that you do not have an answer. You may even have to agree to disagree with the person offering the criticism. This includes organizational criticism you receive through social media. By the way, especially during seasons of change, I save my answers to the criticisms I receive because I know I will likely be answering the same criticism again.

I love the scene in *It's a Wonderful Life* in which George Bailey responds to criticism that the Bailey Building and Loan is going to collapse. He was on his way to his honeymoon, yet he stopped by the office because he saw a mob of people going there. He took the criticism seriously, considered the importance of the critics, responded as necessary, attempted to calm their fears, and refocused the crowd on the vision of the building and loan business. What a great leadership example during times of stress!

Obviously, this is an extreme and dramatic example, but it points to a reality that happens every day in every organization. And sometimes it is extreme and dramatic. Many times people simply do not understand, so they complain and criticize. The way a leader responds is critical in these moments, and information is often the key to resolving the concern.

NEVER LET THEM SEE YOU WEAK!

I grew up in an era in which the common mind-set was to never let others see you weak if you wanted to be seen as a man. If you want to display courage, never let them see you cry or show any emotions.

Sadly, this phrase and mind-set carried over to many practices of leadership. Many falsely assumed a strong leader was one who always had control of their emotions. They never displayed a hint of weakness. Even today, many leaders are afraid to be discovered for their inefficiencies and shortcomings.

Thankfully, leadership today is more about being real with people. It is about admitting failure. It is about being transparent about weaknesses. It is about not covering up flaws but exposing them so others can learn from them. It is about being willing to say "I don't know how" or "This is not my area of expertise." It is about a willingness to say "I am afraid" or "I need help with this one."

As we close out this chapter on the myth of popularity, I need to point out that when it comes to being a respected leader today, it is all about authenticity! Let me be clear. I am not suggesting you not try your hardest, not put your best foot forward, or constantly complain about not being able to keep up. I am not at all suggesting you no longer care what people think about you or even whether they like you or not. People want to follow confident, capable leaders.

Plus, there are times, such as moments of crisis, when leaders have to be strong when no one else is. They need to display strength and character in the midst of chaos and turmoil.

In the day-to-day process of leading others, I suggest you not try to be someone you are not. Instead, be honest about who you really are. Humility is an attractive quality in leadership. And I suggest you lead your people toward the best outcome, whether it makes you popular or not.

The goal of leadership is not to make everyone happy. It is to lead people to a better reality than they know today.

 **MYTH 6**

Leaders Must Have Charisma and Be Extroverts

A FEW YEARS AGO I WAS RUNNING IN PHILADELPHIA. IT IS one of my favorite cities in which to run. I love the Fairmount Park System, because I can run for miles in new territory. If you get there early enough, you can run alongside the water while rowing teams from the various area colleges and row clubs do their morning practices.

On this particular day, I set out to explore a multi-mile loop around a portion of the park. Shortly into my run, I entered the park in front of a young coed running at the same pace with me. (I assumed her identity based on the college sweatshirt she was wearing and our proximity to the college.)

We ran for about a half mile, and then she apparently became impatient with my pace and decided to run faster. She gave me a look that seemed to say, "Get out of my way, old man," and quickly disappeared from sight. I continued my steady pace through the park and encountered her again a couple of miles later. She had looped around the park and was heading back, still continuing at her faster pace. We smiled at each other as we passed.

And then the story took a change in my favor.

After three or four miles I returned to the place we had originally met. And who did I see? My coed friend was barely walking, out of breath, holding her stomach to keep from throwing up, and in obvious pain. She could not finish the track.

I realize some people are sprinters and some are long-distance runners. She may have been the former, but I have to be honest—as the old guy—I got a boost in my adrenaline when I was still running with plenty of fuel in my tank.

Now, before you think I am awful, I did not gloat in front of her. I chuckled under my breath, of course. The reason I share this story, though, is that it reminded me of an important leadership principle I discovered years ago: the tortoise and the hare principle. It unpacks something like this.

There are certainly times an organization
needs to sprint. So run like a hare.

Organizations need times of stretching before they can take huge leaps forward. Healthy organizations continue to grow. These times often require fast decisions and the ability to adapt quickly. Change is a constant. Momentum is built when energy and excitement combine and things are running at full speed ahead. Every organization should continually have periods of sprinting.

But this cannot be the only pace of a healthy organization. An organization cannot sustain itself forever at a rapid pace.

There are also times an organization needs
to slow the pace to tortoise speed.

It may sound boring to a driven leader, but the long-term, sustainable health of an organization depends on establishing systems and strategies. And as much as we may resist it, even structure. Yes, structure.

Take a church plant, for example. Initially, it seems like a sprint. Everything is new. Exciting. Fast paced. Everyone has more than one job and no one complains.

Over time, however, to continue to evolve as a healthy church, there comes a need at some point for structure. Systems need to be implemented. There may even be a need for a few rules. Yes, rules. More volunteers need to be recruited and trained, and people need fewer jobs and to become more specialized in what they do.

Even in an established church or organization this is true. As I am writing this, we have come out of several years of rapid growth. Knowing the principle of the tortoise and the hare, we decided not to add an additional service at this time, even though we need one according to all normal church growth measures. Knowing our energy could only be spread so far, we knew this would allow us to launch some new initiatives to take our people deeper in their walk with Christ.

As one who prefers growth, this was a difficult decision for me. The fact is, most of us—that is, leader types—would rather sprint than slow down the pace. I wished I could have sprinted on that day in Philadelphia. It can almost become cool to be sprinting, so much so that we never really attain a healthy foundation on which to build long-term, sustainable growth.

And hopefully all of us ultimately want to finish well. We want to go the distance. This requires us to learn to pace ourselves like a tortoise.

You cannot sprint forever.

I wish I could devote the rest of this chapter to the need for rest in our lives and in the organizations we lead. I will address that on a personal level later, but God knew we needed it enough to include a Sabbath in the Ten Commandments. In fact, if you need to, take a nap before you finish this chapter. When you're ready, we'll continue.

I opened with the running story and discussed sprinting and resting for three reasons. First, I love the story and it gives us another leadership principle. Second, there will be a tendency to skip this chapter as soon as you think you know what it is about if you are an extrovert. I get it, but I encourage you not to do so. In fact, depending on how much of an extrovert you are, this may be the most important chapter for you. Third, it helps introduce this sixth myth of leadership: leaders must be extroverted charismatics.

And all the introverts said, "Amen!"

Just as the fastest one does not always win the race, the most extroverted is not always the best leader for the team.

COMMONALITY OF LEADERSHIP

There are many things leaders have in common. There are things in a church or organization that are determined by leaders regardless of whether they are extroverted charismatics or extremely introverted.

One of my mentors said, "Everything rises and falls on leadership." He did not make this up, but he somehow learned in his seventy-plus years of experience how true it is.

In so many ways, leaders set the standard others will follow.

Using the tortoise and hare principle, the first standard is pace.

The speed of change and the speed of work on a team is ultimately set by the leader. If the leader moves too slowly, so moves the team. If the leader moves too quickly, the team will do likewise. Thankfully, I was wise enough to know we needed to slow down a little, at least for a season. We did not need to slow for long, but we were going so fast, things were beginning to be ignored that would later prove harmful to the church in the long term.

There are some other ways the leader sets the standard.

Vision. The senior leader primarily communicates the God-given vision to the people. Others will take it only as seriously as you do. Keeping it ever before the people is primarily in your hands.

Character. The moral value of the church and staff follows closely behind its senior leadership. Our example is Jesus, and none of us fully live out his standard. But the quality of the church's character in every major area of life will closely mirror the depth of the leader's character.

Team spirit. If the leader is not a cheerleader for the team, there will seldom be any cheerleaders on the team. Energy and enthusiasm are often directly proportional to the attitude of the leader.

Generosity. No church—no organization for that matter—will be more generous than its most senior leadership. There may be individuals who are generous, but as a whole, people follow the example of their leadership in this area as much or more than any other.

Completing goals and objectives. The leader does not complete all the tasks (and should not), but ultimately the leader sets the bar on whether goals and objectives are met. Complacency prevails when the leader does not set measurable progress as a value and ensure systems are in place to meet them.

Creativity. The leader does not have to be the most creative person on the team (and seldom is), but the team will be no more creative than the leader allows. A leader who stifles idea generation puts a lid on creativity and eventually curtails growth and change.

Team members will seldom outperform the bar their leader sets for them. Consequently, and why this is so important a discussion, an organization will normally cease to grow beyond the bar the leader sets.

LEADERSHIP IS NOT ABOUT PERSONALITY

Notice what I did not say the leader sets for the team: the personality of the team. Granted, the leader's personality influences the team. It may even impact who the team hires and how people perform on the job. But the leader does not, or at least should not, set the personality for the team. Not everyone should be like the leader, and the leader should not be like everyone on the team.

Years ago I learned that leadership is about influence, not personality.

People have individual personalities. They are unique. Some are detail oriented. Some are not. Some are introverts. Some are extroverts. And everything exists in between.

Just as diverse as the individual members are on a team, so will the leaders of these teams be. They are not all extroverted charismatics. The leader is not always the loudest or even most frequent voice in the room. Granted, they are not all introverted either, but certainly no one personality type has an advantage on providing good leadership.

This particular myth may be one of the most misunderstood—or maybe this is the one myth most applied to me in my leadership. It is one I take personally. We assume all leaders are alike. We assume they have the same disposition and the same approach to life. To be a successful leader, many have the false idea we must be bigger than life, equally engaging and being energized by the people around us.

I cannot tell you how many people I have encountered who were being held back in their leadership because they were not loud-mouthed and charismatic. Okay, I apologize. Loud-mouthed is not a fair assessment. But seriously, some of the best leaders on your team are introverts, and if you are not intentional, you might overlook them and never give them a proper chance to lead.

We tend to script the personality and traits and even physical stature we think a leader should possess. But we have a great biblical example of how the one who seems most logical is not always the best leader. Remember God choosing the less likely to be king? "But the LORD said to Samuel, 'Do not look at his appearance or at his physical stature, because I have refused him. For the LORD does not see as man sees; for man looks at the outward appearance, but the LORD looks at the heart'" (1 Sam. 16:7).

Just as the fastest person does not always win the race, the most extroverted is not always the leader, even of the largest churches or organizations. Being extroverted is not an automatic qualification for being a good leader.

The fact is, however, I know lots of pastors of large churches and leaders of huge organizations, college presidents and elected officials, who are as introverted as I. Some of the best-known preachers are introverts.

My best advice to introverts who desire to lead:

> Do not be stereotyped into being a mythical leader. It is perfectly okay to be you. In fact, it is when you are being yourself that you will be the best at leadership.

I would add, it is okay for me to be me. It has taken me years to understand who God created me to be and then actually live it. I am extremely introverted. The larger our church becomes and the bigger my role of leadership, the more introverted I become.

I am an introvert. Some people can question whether they are or not, but I do not. I am certified to administer the Myers-Briggs[1] personality inventory, so I know the language well. I have studied the concept. It did not require much study for me, though. I am in the camp.

This means I am more tired when I go home on Sundays. This means I avoid certain crowds unless I have a clear purpose for being there. This means I run alone and I am okay with doing so. This means I am probably harder to get to know than some people. I get all this. I own it. It is me.

I am just being candid. Frankly, I would be more comfortable leading by e-mail on some days. I could distribute my thoughts after having plenty of time to think them through. People could reply with theirs. We could have virtual meetings throughout the day via e-mail. But how healthy would such an environment be?

I realize this is a reality for some who work remotely these days, but in our church environment, if I am not seen, it greatly impacts the health of the team.

The struggles of introversion in ministry are real. I do not deny this. Introverts can make great leaders, but it does not mean introverts have it easy. Some of their struggle is due to the misunderstandings, the myth, and some because of the requirements of the job. I work to overcome those limitations, but I cannot ignore them.

FALSE ASSUMPTIONS

What surprises me, however, is how misunderstood introverts sometimes are. There are a lot of false assumptions made when someone is introverted.

I write frequently on my blog about introverts and how to relate to them. A fellow introvert in our church told me his mother-in-law said to him, "I was so glad to read Pastor Ron's post on introversion. Now I better understand your condition." Ha! So it is a condition. Is it a condition like dandruff or like a handicap? How bad a condition is it?

This mother-in-law is one of the sweetest women you could ever meet. She meant nothing by her remark other than encouragement, but it is interesting how people view introversion. This is especially true when the person happens to be a leader—or a pastor. As I stated, I have been told I have no business being a pastor because of my introversion.

Along with the stereotypes come personal challenges in a world and workplace that seem to favor extroversion. The truth is, I have to be uncomfortable at times as a leader and as an introvert. I could have done the children's camp. It would have been awkward and hard, but I would have made it through. I have done other similar things.

There are some downsides to being an introverted leader. The following are just a few.

I hesitate to make the connections I should.

Sometimes I miss opportunities to build my network. The best connection can be in the room, and I will let the moment pass and regret it later. I hate when I do it, but I do.

I am worn out after a long day.

After a day of talking, I need time to rejuvenate. This can impact my family time if I am not careful. It also leads to people at the end of the day telling me how tired I look. Thanks! This is my favorite comment, in case you are wondering. (I am joking, in case you are still wondering.)

I am not as quick-witted in crowds.

People who know me tend to think I have a good sense of humor. I am easy to talk with and fairly quick-witted in comfortable crowds. I have been told I make people feel comfortable, but sometimes I appear awkward on first impressions, when I try to make one. (So if you meet me in public, please give me more than one chance.)

I stress at the pressure to connect.

I realize there is a need to talk with people. It is what I do. It is what I need to do. But wrestling through my introverted tendencies actually adds even more stress to my life. I can be restless the night before a big social event. I can even lose sleep. (How is this for transparency?)

I can keep relationships shallow.

If I am not careful—and thankfully I am fairly disciplined here—I will close out people from really knowing the real me, which could subject me to all kinds of temptations, anxiety, and even depression. The trained counselor in me knows this well, and I see it often among other introverts.

Crowded rooms are intimidating.

Even though I teach every Sunday at a large church, it can be very daunting when I am not in my normal role. I love crowded rooms in terms of reaching people for Christ. The more the merrier. But I have to force myself to engage when it is not something I normally do.

As I was writing this book, I experienced an example of this. We were conducting our annual vacation Bible school (we call it Camp Immanuel). Last year, we decided we wanted to be more intentional and engage parents and invite unchurched families to the church. Specifically, the suggestion was that I would engage them. The plan was for me to be very visible during the week. We would provide some reception activity where parents who wanted to meet me could do so. I was all on board. I love connecting with people who may be looking for a church home. I know part of my pastoral role is to be an ambassador for the church.

Each night began with a worship event. It is big, loud, and engaging. Most of the children love the jumping and dancing. There is lots of energy in the room, which is key to understanding this story.

During the week of Camp Immanuel, my assistant reminded me of my commitment. The only difference was, in addition to the reception idea, I was asked to welcome parents from the stage during the worship part of the evening—during the high-energy, engaging part of the evening! I would not need to dance (thankfully), but I knew I would need to be high energy.

Hence my dilemma: I am not an extroverted charismatic leader.

The morning of the day I was supposed to do the welcome, I woke up with my stomach in knots. I was nervous all day. Granted, I speak to thousands of people every week, and I get nervous doing that. But not this nervous. This was different, because the expectation was different. I was to be engaging on demand, entertaining perhaps, in a room filled with energy. Ugh! I wish it were not so tough for me.

And right now you know how weird I can be.

As the time approached, our children's pastor asked me if I

still wanted to do the welcome. I told him I did not know I had a choice. He said, "Sure, I was just offering if you wanted to do it." Instantly I felt the energy returning to my body that had been missing all day. Relief!

If you are an extrovert, you probably think I am crazy. You may even think, as some have when I have posted about introversion, that I am not qualified to be a pastor. If I wanted to pass up an opportunity to get on stage at Camp Immanuel, why should I be a senior leader of the church? But there rests the myth.

MISUNDERSTANDINGS

Those are honest assessments of myself as an introvert. The misunderstandings people have about introverts, however, are astounding and sometimes even hurtful. Here are a few that have been cast my way and toward fellow introverts:

We are all the same.

While all introverts are reserved, constantly quiet, and unsocial, introverts are nevertheless a diverse group, with varying degrees of introversion. For example, if you give me the authority, I will lead the meeting. No problem. But this would never be comfortable for some introverts.

We are shy.

This may be your word, but it is not mine. I prefer *purposeful*. Others may call it something else. I talk when there is a purpose. I am not afraid to do so. Three-year-olds are shy when they hide behind their daddy. That is not me.

We need more courage.

Why I oughta . . . (You will get this sarcasm only if you are a Three Stooges fan.) Seriously, I'm not chicken when I choose not to speak. I am being comfortable with who I am.

We have nothing to say.

Actually I have lots to say. After all, I blog almost daily. I did a daily devotional for more than a dozen years, and I had a radio program for seventeen years. Have you ever seen how often I update Twitter and Facebook? I have plenty to say. Sometimes I do and sometimes I do not express it, but often how I choose to communicate will be different from how others choose to communicate.

We are not as intelligent, because we do not speak as much.

Yeah, in a lot of ways I am ignorant. It was not until I was about fifty years old that I began to understand all I do not know. I am not trying to be funny, but in some ways I am smarter than the guy who never quits talking. (You know the one.) I am less likely to say the thing I wish I had not said because I did not think before I talked. It happens with me, too, but not as often as it might for some.

We are arrogant, aloof, or unfriendly.

I am a lot of negative things. Those are not really the main three. People who know me tend to call me humble, though I am not necessarily humble. I have just been humbled by life. And so I am not looking down on anyone. I sometimes, though, have to go back and apologize once I hear that someone thinks

I avoided them. This happens especially with extremely extroverted people.

Honestly, I love everyone. Or at least my biblical commitment and personal goal is to do so. Whether or not I talk to you will not be a good determinant of whether or not I like you. It might even mean I respect you enough to listen more than speak.

We need you to talk for us.

Um, actually we would rather you not. This said, I sometimes let my wife talk for me. She is good at it too. But if I have an opinion I think needs sharing, I can speak for myself. Or I can regret later that I did not. But either way, please do not try to be my voice.

We need to change, mature, or grow as a person.

I have heard this so many times, mostly about other leaders someone is trying to coach and asking for my advice about. Wrong. Introversion is not a maturity problem. They may need to mature in how they respond as a leader, but they do not need to mature in personality. The truth is, I am quieter than some leaders you know—or your perception of a leader—but my personality has not changed a ton in all the years I have been leading. There are lots of things wrong with me. Introversion is not one of them.

So if it is not a problem of personality, you may be wondering how to better engage introverts in your leadership. My best advice for leaders about engaging people in meetings would not be to consider them to be introverts but simply to consider that everyone is different. I addressed this in chapter 3. When it comes to meeting dynamics, everyone has something to add and does so in their own way.

Part of my job, if I am leading a meeting, is to analyze the people in the room as much as I can before the meeting begins. If the meeting involves people you do not know or know well, it is more difficult, but good leaders study people, such as the way they respond to others before meetings, when they are introducing themselves, or their posture during meetings.

I do understand, however, the question of engaging introverts. Many introverts do not engage in meetings. They keep to themselves, especially in large group settings. They are not as easy to get to know. And, yes, even I can be this way, especially if I am not in the leadership position at the meeting, having to force myself out of my introversion—or if it is a meeting full of extroverts.

ENGAGING INTROVERTS

So here is my answer to some of the questions about engaging introverts in meetings. Again, we are not all alike, even though we share a characteristic. Try a few of these and see if they improve your meeting dynamics.

Give them time to respond.

This is huge. Introverts typically reflect inward, so they respond only after they have thought through an answer. This is a great characteristic if used well, because it usually means their answer has already been tested in their mind. They are likely to share some of the most valid options on the table if you give the process time to work.

Ask specific questions—ahead of time.

Give them a problem and time to solve it, and most introverts, if left alone, will enjoy the challenge. If you want them to brainstorm effectively, tell them exactly what you are going to brainstorm about prior to the meeting.

Let them respond in writing.

When I know there are numerous introverts in a group, I will find a way to let them put their thoughts down in writing. I have even allowed them to text or e-mail me during the meeting. It is amazing some of the suggestions I have received when an introvert does not have to speak aloud.

Do not put them on the spot.

If you call on them for an immediate response, you might get an answer. That said, it will not usually be their best answer, and it will often keep them from ever sharing again. Introverts are not huge fans of being singled out to answer a question. They may be better prepared if you ask a question and let people who have instant answers (usually extroverts) respond first, and then call on the introverts later.

Separate them from the most extroverted.

If there are too many extroverts in the group, introverts are more likely to shut down communication. Try putting a group of introverts together, give them plenty of time and thought provokers to stimulate conversation, and allow the process to work on their time. Then prepare to be amazed.

Give them an assignment they can control.

Many introverts (me included) can perform tasks if we are put in seats of responsibility. It could be speaking to a group or working the crowd at a banquet, but when it is purposeful and I have an assigned responsibility, and I can control how I do it, I am more likely to perform like an extrovert. Before you have the meeting, and if they are willing, give introverts an assignment for which they are responsible for sharing.

Express genuine and specific interest in their ideas.

Introverts, like all of us, love to be respected for their thoughts and ideas. If you want an introvert to share more, remind them how valuable they are to the team and how much their thoughts are needed. This is best done before the meeting starts.

As already stated, this is not an exact science. We are all different. Knowing introversion, however, as I do, it is a little easier for me to land on these points. Do not overlook the introverts on your team as if they have nothing to add to your discussions. They do. They will simply share that information differently than the extroverts do. They may not talk as much as some or seem to have as many opinions, but when they do, it will often be golden.

SUGGESTIONS FOR INTROVERTS

Perhaps you are an introverted leader. After a post on intro-version, Marvin, the pastor of a small but growing church, e-mailed me. He was surprised I admitted to my introversion. After some things said to him recently, and with the expectations he felt being placed on him from the church, he was questioning if he was a good fit for the ministry.

As I listened to some of the expectations laid on Marvin, they seemed totally unrealistic. They wanted a pastor to have a scheduled week of coffee shop–type meetings with all the groups in the church. Monday might be the men's group at McDonald's. On Tuesday the lady's knitting club wanted him to visit with them. Wednesday was a local civic club several members attended and the seniors' prayer group. (I am mak-ing up the groups from memory, but it was literally something every day.) The previous pastor had been wonderful at this. He loved to talk to everyone. Based on what I know about the church, I am not sure this was the best use of the previous pas-tor's time, but for introverted Marvin, it was near impossible. Adding these socials to the things Marvin already had to do as pastor, he simply could not keep up the routine.

I coached Marvin with some thoughts on responding to the church as an introverted pastor.

Love people.

This sounds simple and may even sound trite—plus Marvin already knew this and agreed—but I genuinely love people. I love connecting with people. I want to engage with others. Doing so does not come naturally to me, but it is not because I do not love them. In fact, I think it is very hard to be a leader—and certainly a pastor—unless you love people. (One of the biggest misunderstandings of introverts is when extroverts think we do not love people because of the way we respond to people. It is not true for most of us.) My advice to Marvin was to respond to people out of his love for them, which led me to the next point.

Be purposeful.

Since I love people and know connecting with them is a huge part of my position, I remind myself there is a reason to be extroverted in some occasions. Often people are waiting on me to engage them. To be a kingdom builder, I have to converse with others even when it is uncomfortable. The reason I am willing to act outside my comfort zone is that I love people and value having a connection with them more than I love my individual preference or comfort.

Part of being purposeful is to use my energy where it will do the most good. For example, it might be great to occasionally connect with the men at McDonald's, but I am not confident doing so every week will grow the kingdom any faster than doing it every now and then. You have to do the things that produce the greatest long-term results.

Prepare mentally.

I have to prep myself before Sunday. I remind myself that I have a job to do, and people are expecting me to engage with them. It is not going to be easy, but "I can do all things through Christ who strengthens me" (Phil. 4:13). It is a mental exercise before any event where I need to be outgoing. (And some days I do better than others.) I also try to plan fewer social events so I can shut down mentally on Saturday evening. Plus, I plan to have adequate recovery time after an extremely extroverted event.

Discipline myself.

At some point, I just do it. I simply have to make myself do what I may not at first want to do. This means that every Sunday I work the room to make connections with the people I do not know, build new relationships, or strengthen existing ones. With practice, it gets easier. It really does. I am always glad when I engage with people.

Reward myself.

After an extremely extroverted occasion, I crash heartily. Sunday afternoon naps are the deepest sleeping I have ever had. My family understands if I am quieter than normal at Sunday lunch. Sometimes I go for a run. Sometimes I plan a walk with Cheryl. It is my time to renew so I can do it again when needed.

The introvert myth is not true. You can be an introvert and be a leader, even a very good leader, of small and large churches and organizations.

As I close out this chapter, you may be analyzing your team to see who the introverted people are. Chances are good your gut is correct, but all you probably have to do is ask. Most introverts—especially those who are extremely introverted—know this is part of their personality. It never hurts, and it is usually helpful, to do an assessment with your team, such as the Myers-Briggs[2] personality inventory. It will be useful to identify those on your team who are the most introverted.

As I said, if it is required, I can be the bigger-than-life, extroverted, and charismatic person in the room. Certainly I am more extroverted on Sunday mornings.

In high school, as student body president, I had one goal: I wanted to increase the level of school spirit we had as Northeast Eagles. We were a new high school. I began attending in my junior year. Two high schools had been merged into one. Seniors had an option to attend their original high school, but everyone else was forced to attend the new school. Except for some of the freshmen, we basically had one thing in common: we did not want to be at this new school. We had left our friends. We were forced to change our allegiance. It did not seem fair to any of us.

I would have done almost anything to increase school spirit. I often led at pep rallies. I tried to be funny every day with the morning announcements. I put on my happy face every day in the hallways, trying to be contagious with enthusiasm. I was extremely extroverted, bigger-than-life most days. It was not always comfortable, but it was always strategic.

The most charismatic thing I did was during the Miss Northeast Beauty Pageant. They had announced a special guest would be appearing in an attempt to get more students to attend. There were rumors floating about which celebrity might be there, so I am certain there was disappointment but also lots of laughs when I came from behind the curtain dressed in a tutu. I do not remember much about the evening (I think selective memories are good), but I do remember the shock on my mother's face, who did not know I was going to do it.

I am not sure my strategy was moved any further with this guest appearance, but for one night we had some unity—even if it was laughter at my expense. The point is, I was a leader with a mission and I would have done anything to help develop school spirit.

No doubt there have been times in your life when you believed in someone or something in spite of your fears, the possibility of rejection or even persecution, and you were willing to accept the challenge and defend that person or cause. Surely parents feel this way about their children.

This is what leaders do every day. Personality does not motivate them to take the risks of leadership. What truly inspires them is the pursuit of something they perceive to be valuable enough to be worth leading people to achieve it. All leaders have this in common.

 **MYTH 7**

Leaders Accomplish by Controlling Others

CHAPTER 1 BEGAN WITH THE STORY OF MY FIRST LEADER-ship position. It seems appropriate for this last chapter to add to that.

I was promoted several times at the company until I led one of the larger sales divisions in the department store. After I completed management training and served in every department in the store, I was placed over the men's and boy's departments. By this time I had learned some good leadership principles, but foundational to who I was as a leader was (and is) my faith. I believe in treating people with dignity and respect, even when they may not be performing up to expectations.

Our division of the company was merged with a larger division, and our senior corporate leadership changed. It was obvious after the first few meetings that we had different philosophies of leading people. This became most apparent during a sales review meeting.

To understand what happened, you need a little background. Our store was in a military town, so we had a large population of soldiers and their families. This was during the first Gulf War and large numbers of these soldiers were deployed. Their deployments were long, so many of the families left the area and returned to their hometowns, where they would be closer to family. Our sector of the city often looked like a ghost town.

It is important to know that 90 percent of our deployed soldiers were male. They accounted for nearly 50 percent of sales in the men's department, of which I was the leader. They were nearly seven thousand miles away from our store. Our sales took a major hit.

I was soon summoned to a meeting with the new division leaders, who started drilling me as to why I had allowed sales to plummet in my department. None of my reasons seemed satisfactory to them. They did not want to hear about my goals for next year, after the troops had returned. I was told that I needed new employees who were better at sales. They told me to be tougher on my current employees and push them to drive sales higher.

At one tense point in the meeting, the most senior leader in the room stood up and threw my sales book (a large spiral notebook) across the table and into my chest. I was a fairly skinny guy, and it hurt. He yelled some harsh words my mother never let me say and stormed out of the room, saying, "You better get some better answers, boy, or we are going in a different direction in leadership!"

I had been with the company almost ten years at this point.

I was once recognized as one of the top five employees out of over twenty-five thousand employees. I was a leader in sales for many years. Things had changed. And it all had to do with a change in leadership.

This is, of course, an extreme example, but I learned from this experience that I never wanted to be a controlling, domineering leader. Such leadership simply does not work. And it is not a biblical way to lead.

I can sense some pushback. I get it every time I talk about this leadership myth. How could we ever get anything done in an organization unless someone controls things so they do?

If you are pushing back about how things get accomplished without controlling leadership, you obviously did not read chapter 4, where I addressed delegation. (Sorry to call you out like this, but seriously, go back and read it now if you need to.) I mentioned there are times a leader needs to control, although I used the term *micromanage*.

The problem with controlling leadership, besides the fact that it does not work in bringing out the best in people, is that it produces horrible overall results for the organization.

Three things happen in an organization under a controlling leader.

LEADERS LEAVE

You simply cannot keep a real leader when you try to control them. Period. At the very least, you will not keep them for long. To complete the story above, the company did not have to seek a change in direction of leadership. I gave it to them. Shortly after this encounter—and a few others like it—I resigned my position.

I find this especially true among the younger set of leaders entering the workforce today. Leaders need room to breathe, explore, and take risks. Controlling leadership, however, stifles people. Genuine leaders will look for places they can grow.

Taylor is a bright young leader. Since I have gotten to know him, I have wanted to give him a position on my team. He has a tremendously bright future in ministry and leadership, and the only thing standing in his way of leading a large church is age and experience. He will be there someday.

Taylor took a job as a youth pastor at a church right out of seminary. He had served two previous churches in part-time roles, but this was his first full-time vocational job. He was so excited about the opportunity to experiment with some of the ideas he had for reaching students, many of which he developed while he was a student himself, but also during his two recent jobs and his seminary training.

The church was so excited about Taylor. They recruited him through some mutual connections. They courted him, encouraged him, and made him feel incredibly welcome. The students and parents were open to change and excited about the potential they saw in Taylor.

There was only one problem: Taylor's boss.

(I do not like the word *boss*, but from everything Taylor shared with me, it is the most appropriate term in his situation.)

Taylor reported to one of the more senior members of the church staff. This guy had been around the church most of his career. He was well respected, loved by the church, and was, by all appearances, a hard worker. The only problem was how he managed the people reporting directly to him. He was a tyrant.

Okay, maybe *tyrant* is too harsh a word. And maybe in full disclosure, I have a certain bias against controlling leaders, and maybe it stems from the scars on my chest from a thick sales book being thrown into it. Dictionary.com defines tyrant as "a sovereign or other ruler who uses power oppressively or unjustly." Maybe this is not quite the way this guy leads, but it is certainly close.

Long story short, Taylor started looking for a new opportunity six months into his new job.

FOLLOWERS STAY

The second thing that happens in an organization as a result of controlling leadership is some followers will stay.

I need to pause here and assure you that I believe we are all leaders at some level. It may be in our homes, neighborhoods, or workplaces. It might be situational, positional, or relational. It might be a seasonal or permanent position of leadership. We all have influence over other people in some way. But we need good followers too. And great organizations and churches are built on the backs of the people who are willing to follow another person's leadership. Praise God for good followers!

Controlling leadership can keep those who follow the rules, who are dogmatically loyal, and those who like to please others. You can find controlling leaders who appear to have huge flocks of dedicated servant followers. They stay because they have a sense of responsibility, not because they love the style of leadership. Many followers have served under controlling leadership for so long that they do not realize there is any other kind of leadership. Often, too, their fear of venturing out on their own keeps them under the leader's control. In my experience, most often their work life is unfulfilled and they are often miserable, but they do not know how to do anything about it.

One thing I have loved about the last two churches I have pastored is the number of ministers who come to our church to rest, heal, and reenergize while in between vocational positions. We invite them to attend our staff meetings. We try to give them ministry opportunities. We assist them as best we can in finding their next place of service.

Mike was one of these pastors. He had served in a worship leadership role at his previous church under a controlling leader. Mike's personality is more of a follower, but he is a tremendous relational leader. He had been extremely loyal to the pastor in spite of the man's controlling tendencies. I doubt anyone in the church even knew that Mike had problems with the pastor's leadership style. He was just that kind of guy.

Mike had been at the church nearly two decades and hoped to finish his career there. But one day the pastor decided it was time for a change. In an effort to reach a younger demographic, he wanted to change the worship style of the church. In his mind, the only way to do this was to change the worship pastor. Mike had been extremely loyal to the pastor, but he soon found out the pastor was not equally loyal to Mike—which is something else I have observed about controlling leaders.

The team had grown to like Mike and invited him to be part of more events with the staff. He went to lunch with the staff, participated in brainstorming sessions, and even attended a conference with us. After one of our meetings, a staff member told me Mike had asked him, "Will you be honest with me? Is all this for real?" He could not believe a staff really could enjoy their work as much as the team seemed to enjoy theirs. At his previous church, Mike had stayed out of loyalty, but he was never fulfilled as a leader.

ORGANIZATIONS STALL

The real detriment of controlling leadership is it always limits the organization to the strengths, dreams, and abilities of the controlling leader. One person, one leader can only control so much. They can only control so many people or tasks. This is one of the leading reasons we see churches plateau and a business's growth stagnate. Controlling leadership keeps people from developing as leaders themselves, and it robs the organization of their leadership potential.

I have tried throughout this book to be honest about my own shortcomings. I could easily be a controlling leader.

StrengthsFinder, which is a popular assessment for measuring a person's talents, assigns Command as my top strength each of the several times I have taken it. Consider how their website describes this strength: "People with strong Command talents naturally take charge. They see what needs to be done, and they are willing to speak up. . . . People with strong Command bring decisiveness and emotional clarity. They have the ability to bring to light what is often avoided or unstated. This gives them the ability to resolve conflicts and misunderstandings."[1] It adds, "There are times when you need to manage your compulsion to take over. Let situations unfold without always feeling like you need to step in."[2]

I have learned StrengthsFinder is equally helpful at discovering areas where you are not as strong or where your strengths could be a problem in leading well, but it does seem to put a nice spin on even those areas. I think the warning it is trying to give people wired like me is something like this: if you are not careful, you will run over the people who get in your way!

I have to discipline myself in this area of my leadership. And I do this in several ways.

I SUBMIT TO OTHERS ON OUR TEAM

We need good leadership, because without leadership and a big-picture perspective, nothing of great value ever happens. But as much as leadership is important, nothing of great value ever happens without good followers.

You cannot lead well and be a control freak at the same time. You need to solicit buy-in from others. You need to collaborate. You need to process the success rate of the change you are aiming for and recalibrate as needed. You have to delegate, and this means you must release your perceived right to determine the exact way something is done. Progress toward a goal must be more important than the exact actions taken in order to achieve the goal.

So at times, really many times, I submit my authority to the people who are supposedly looking to me for leadership. There are at least seven things that induce me to submit to the people I should be leading.

1. *When I have no strong feeling.* If nothing inside me says this is wrong or if I have no strong opinion about it, I yield to someone on the team who shows they have a strong passion for the goal. I trust their gut.

2. *When they know more than I do.* This happens more often than you might imagine. I try to surround myself with people who are smarter than me in different areas. Why would I not rely on them for their expertise?

3. *When I want to give them an opportunity.* Be honest. Releasing authority to others might be an opportunity for them to fail. This is perhaps the primary reason some leaders never delegate authority. But sometimes the only way we learn is by trying and falling short. Some of the best discoveries are learned in this way.

4. *When they have thought about it more than I have.* Often we try to lead people through muddy waters. The path is not clear. There are so many things that happen within our church (and probably your church) where I simply do not have the time to commit to processing everything. I have to trust other people. Sometimes I have to yield to other people because they have more time invested in an issue than I and can help steer us to clarity better than I.

5. *When they have to live more directly with the consequences.* If it is more about their individual area of ministry or

responsibility, and does not impact other areas of the church, then I am likely to delegate authority to them.

6. *When I am already overwhelmed.* To be effective as a leader—and to last for the long haul—I need to recognize I can only do what I can do. I have to trust the people with whom God has surrounded me to do what they can do. And I know I need their help to prioritize my best efforts toward the things only I can do.

7. *Whenever I can.* Seriously. Good leadership involves empowerment. It is about delegating authority and allowing people to grow in their responsibility. So when I have the opportunity, I will let other people make decisions without my input.

It is important to understand that I am delegating my authority, not relegating my authority. I mentioned the difference earlier. I am not diminishing the fact I am the senior leader and ultimately responsible for the overall vision and direction of our church. (Under God's authority, of course.) My team needs to know they are not alone. I am close if they need my help, and I will support them in the decisions they make.

I COLLABORATE WITH OTHERS

I am an idea person. I have a million of them. I wish we got paid for ideas alone. I would be a wealthy guy. I am far better at coming up with ideas than I am at implementing them, which is probably why I am not a wealthy guy.

When I have an idea, because I know I could command it to happen, I invite other people into the discussion. I give the team the right to challenge my ideas or me. If I did not, we would get into some serious trouble.

I had a random idea that we should consider launching Saturday night services. In our community, there is currently no strong presence of Saturday night services. And the few who did have Saturday services have canceled them for a variety of good reasons. One had a change of focus, one lost their pastor—stuff like that.

The control tendency in me would have called the staff together, unpacked my idea, appointed a special team to coordinate all the particulars, and set a date when it was to start. Done. Saturday night services would be launched and I would simply have to show up to preach.

And while this method of empowerment may seem effective—and it sounds basically like what we did and how I mostly operate in leadership—when you hear the end of the story, you will know why I am glad I did not simply control the launch of our Saturday night services.

Knowing my ideas can sometimes be really bad, the idea I presented to the team was actually more specific than simply launching Saturday night services. I suggested we do a trial run of three services on Saturday night, each at 5 P.M., leading up to Easter, with the third Saturday being Easter weekend. We would call it an experiment. (I have found this is a great way to test something and often you encounter less resistance if it doesn't sound permanent.)

I invited the lead staff to evaluate my idea. I gave them

freedom to poke holes in the plan. They asked lots of questions. They wanted to clearly know the purpose. Was it strictly to increase attendance? Who would be our target audience? How would it impact Sunday mornings? How would it impact the staff? (They may not know this, but I would have refused to move forward had we not been unanimous around the idea. When they read this, I hope it will not stop us from doing more experiments in the future.)

So what happened? The three Saturday nights went on the calendar. Our communications team did an outstanding job of promoting the services. We were excited and ready for the anticipated crowds. Our team really believed this was a great idea.

A couple of days before the first Saturday night service, the University of Kentucky basketball team was scheduled to play in a tournament at 5 P.M. *What!* Have you ever lived in a basketball town? Have you ever lived in the University of Kentucky basketball town? Because Louisville is our closest rival, I cannot wear the color red at Christmastime. This town bleeds blue.

Two hundred fifty people attended the first Saturday night service. I realize this is a good-sized church for most people, but when your worship center holds over seventeen hundred, it looks like a very small crowd. We were hoping for six to seven hundred people.

Two days before the next Saturday night service, the Wildcats were scheduled to play on Saturday at 5:15 P.M. *What!* The city was abuzz with basketball. Saturday night came, and we had two hundred people in the room. And this was by Baptist counting. (We always count high!)

Thankfully, there was no basketball game on Easter weekend, and we had a strong crowd of more than six hundred people.

Regardless of the attendance, the experiment helped us learn a few things we would not have known otherwise. First, we can do a Saturday night service. We can do one well, and based on who attended, one is probably needed in our community. Second, Saturday is an option for special occasions. We will likely never have an Easter weekend without one, but we cannot do it in our current structure. I normally work six days a week, so during this experiment I did not have a day off for twenty-seven days. Other staff members were equally impacted.

The biggest lesson for us was if we are going to do Saturday nights, we would have to live with schedule conflicts. Something tells me the University of Kentucky is going to keep on playing basketball. And if you know anything about Lexington, Kentucky, they play to win.

But the greatest thing I learned—far greater than the others listed—was really something I already knew. I was not alone in this decision. When we expected six hundred people and only two hundred came, I was not alone. When my Saturday nights were interrupted for three weeks, I was not alone. It may have been my idea, but there was a shared consensus. No one said, "I told you it wouldn't work" or "I never wanted to do this." I had not controlled the launch of our Saturday night service experiment. Other people on the team had ownership.

If I had exerted controlling leadership over the matter, I would have been left standing alone—or at least feeling alone—and probably like we had failed in some way with the experiment. Instead, we were energized and thankful for all we learned and the chance to explore new opportunities for ministry.

I MAKE LOTS OF WHIPS

Controlling leaders have an even greater tendency to try to control people during times of conflict. How many times have you said or done something in anger and regretted it later? I once fired a good employee in anger. I have always regretted that.

To discipline myself from this one, I have learned to make whips. This one needs a little explanation, but it is one of the most powerful and helpful principles I have ever learned in leadership. It is absolutely vital for those with a tendency toward controlling.

Some lessons you learn the hard way in life and leadership. This one I learned from Jesus. Many years ago, Scripture convicted me. (Is this not what Scripture is supposed to do?) I had read John 2:13–16 many times before, but I saw something this time I had never previously noticed. See if you catch it:

> Now the Passover of the Jews was at hand, and Jesus went up to Jerusalem. And He found in the temple those who sold oxen and sheep and doves, and the money changers doing business. When He had made a whip of cords, He drove them all out of the temple, with the sheep and the oxen, and poured out the changers' money and overturned the tables. And He said to those who sold doves, "Take these things away! Do not make My Father's house a house of merchandise!"

Did you catch it? Did you see the powerful leadership principle about responding in anger? Yes? If so, then you were convicted, too, most likely. It is huge. It will change the way you deal with people in tense or confrontational environments. It will help you to not be controlling. If you did not catch it, read it one more time. This time, I'll add a little emphasis:

> Now the Passover of the Jews was at hand, and Jesus went up to Jerusalem. And He found in the temple those who sold oxen and sheep and doves, and the money changers doing business. *When He had made a whip of cords*, He drove them all out of the temple, with the sheep and the oxen, and poured out the changers' money and overturned the tables. And He said to those who sold doves, "Take these things away! Do not make My Father's house a house of merchandise!"

He made a whip. Before Jesus cleared out the temple, he made a whip—a handcrafted whip. (Imagine what this whip would sell for at auction today.)

Have you ever made a whip out of cords, a whip strong enough to drive out people bent on making money through unrighteous means? I have to be honest. I have never made a whip in my life. I do not know how long it took to make whips in Jesus' day, but it certainly was not instantaneous.

While he made a whip, Jesus had time for reflection. Time to think. Time to process. Time to make a plan. Time to pray.

Suddenly, the scene I had in my head of Jesus seeing the activity in the temple and going wild with anger was not the same. I pictured Jesus sitting on the steps of the temple, talking to his Father. (Scripture says he did nothing except what the Father told him.)

Maybe his thoughts went something like this:

Father, how do you want me to respond to this? They are in the temple . . . money-changing. I know how you feel about that. This is your house. It's supposed to be a House of Prayer. What should I do? How serious should I take this?

[As he twists the leather a little tighter.] You know, Dad, they are going to be writing about this for a very long time. They will teach about it in Bible studies. This scene may even appear in the movies someday. Ron may even put this story in his bestselling book on leadership myths.

Okay, he did not say this last thing, but I thought it would be neat to throw it in. He does know my name though, thankfully.

I can picture Jesus saying, "Help me know how to respond."

The point is that the cleansing of the temple was not a rash decision. It was not unrehearsed. Jesus did not respond purely out of emotion. He was not simply controlling the situation. He certainly could have—he is God.

To me, the cleansing of the temple has the appearance of being a calculated, methodical, strategic move.

Over the years of my leadership experience, since I realized how Jesus actually cleared the temple and faced lots of critics and conflicts of my own, I have made a lot of figurative whips. Perhaps someday I will even make a real one and hang it on my wall. I have taken time before responding to think, process, and develop a plan—all in a spirit of prayer.

The process of being more calculated, methodical, and strategic has made me a better leader. It has helped me to respond to situations better. It has made my leadership style less controlling and more relational.

Shortly after I arrived at an established church, I led the church in sprucing up the building. We needed to clean and paint the walls and redo the landscaping, none of which had been touched in years. There was a spirit of excitement as we prepared, anticipating what visitors would see in the weeks ahead.

A few days into a long week of this process, I was working on my Sunday message in my office when the phone rang. It was a staff member. "Pastor, can you come down to the front of the church? Some of the seniors are upset."

"Well," I replied, "what are they upset about this week?"

"They are not happy with some of the shrubs being cut back out front."

My first thought was, *You have got to be kidding me!*

I left my studies and walked toward the front of the church. My office was a good way from the front door, and it is a large building, but I decided to take an even longer route so I would have a few minutes to reflect on how I would respond.

You know what I did? I made a whip.

I talked to God. I prayed for wisdom. I calmed my initial emotions of frustration and even anger.

I walked out to the front door of the church and listened to their complaint. They thought the shrubs were being cut back too much. Apparently the shrubs had always covered part of the windows.

I said, "I am sorry. I understand you are upset, but there

is something you need to know. I realize I am the new guy, so you don't know this about me yet. You see, I reflected as I walked down here, and to my knowledge I have never in my life planned landscaping. As I recall, I may have nodded approval a couple of times at a nursery and I've cut a few shrubs in my life—not very well, but I did cut them. I didn't know these shrubs were supposed to cover part of the window, and I didn't determine how far the shrubs would be cut. So I had nothing to do with this decision. Here's what I'm going to suggest. You tell us the height they need to be, because I think we all agree they need to be cut and shaped. So you pick the height, because here's what I'm going to do. I'm going to go back to my office and finish preparing the sermon for Sunday, because this is why God called me to your church. Have a great day."

And I walked away.

A couple of days later one of the men stopped me in the hall and apologized for their actions. To this day I am not sure what height those shrubs were or how tall they are now. We have made so many changes in four years, they may not even be there anymore. But it does not seem to matter anyway.

The point is this: I could have controlled the situation. I probably had enough clout as the new guy and enough leadership savvy to get the shrubs cut to any height we wanted in front of the building. Plus, there may be times I need to control the situation. Jesus certainly controlled the situation in the clearing of the temple. And apparently he needed to, and God led him to do it. But in the process of making a whip, God led me toward a different approach. The height of the shrubs was not a big deal in the grand scheme of what we were trying to accomplish. Winning this battle might have crippled me when it came to the bigger changes we needed to make.

Here is the other thing I discovered. Often, once I have made the whip, I do not need to use it. In fact, and here is the real life lesson, sometimes the process has led me to understand I was the one who was wrong. Ouch!

When you are facing conflict in life and leadership, when you are angry, take time to make a whip. It changes everything.

ARE YOU GUILTY?

At this point you might be wondering if you have a tendency to be a controlling leader. Or maybe you're wondering what controlling leadership is. What does it even look like? I have always had a strong personality, but I cannot say I have always understood my tendency to control people. The following are seven warning signs that you may be a controlling leader.

1. *Your team struggles to share new ideas.*

Are people sheepish around you when they have an idea that may be different from yours? Do they apologize prior to approaching you with a new idea? Do they appear timid, fearful, and even reluctant to share a thought? This may be on them, but it might be on you, leader.

2. *You think you are wonderful.*

I am not trying to be funny, and I do not mean to say you are necessarily arrogant or narcissistic. When a leader is in a controlling position, because of their own confidence, they can often believe everyone approves of all they are doing. A controlling leader may not really know how people feel about them. They assume everyone approves of their leadership.

3. *You always know you are right.*

Because you are, right? Seriously, if you never question your own judgment, if you never even think you need to get another's opinion on your ideas, you might be a controlling leader.

4. *You control information.*

Do you enjoy controlling how much anyone else knows, making sure they know less than you? Do you like to be in the power position, that is, if information is power? (And it is.) If you control the information, you will almost always control what is done with it. And you might just be a controlling leader.

5. *You are part of every decision.*

Do you think you should be involved in all the decision-making of your church or organization? Seriously. Be honest. A controlling leader cannot stand when they are not part of the final decision, especially if it proves to be a good one. Similarly, they cannot stand it if people get credit for something in which they had no part.

If you still cannot see whether or not you are a controlling leader, use the following scenario and judge for yourself how you would feel. A decision is made. It is genius. Everyone applauds the decision, but because of your level of involvement, you are on the sidelines, getting no recognition. How do you feel?

6. *You cannot let go of the reins.*

Do you fear others being in control of a project? Does it make you nervous? Do you feel the need to continually step in and check on things? I am not suggesting a leader delegates and disappears. That is not good leadership either. But if you can never let someone be the primary leader of a task, you might be a controlling leader. One of the main reasons leaders control is because they feel out of control when they do not.

7. *You are the final authority on every decision.*

Think for a minute about the decisions made in your organization over the last year or even the last month. Did you have to sign off on all of them? Were there any significant decisions made in which you were not part of the process? Be honest.

Controlling is not really leadership. It is closer to dictatorship. Effective leaders encourage others to lead. They challenge people to be creative and take ownership and responsibility for accomplishing the vision. They learn to delegate through empowerment.

RESPONDING TO THE BOSS

I realize some readers are on the other side of this discussion. You are serving under a controlling leader. What can you do? What if you desire to stay in your position, you are not happy with being controlled as you are currently, but you do not know what to do? There are three things you can do in response to a controlling leader.

Quit

People have challenged me and pointed out that winners never quit, but I disagree. If you were placed in a position by a call of God, this may not be an option until God releases you—and I would consider the other two options before considering this option—but sometimes the best thing for the individual and the organization is for everyone to make a fresh start. And there is nothing to be ashamed of if this is indeed the only option.

Quitting should not be a rash or vindictive decision. You should attempt to leave on the best terms possible, because you simply may not mesh with this particular leadership style. To be true to yourself and have integrity, you may have to seek another environment that allows you to better grow as a leader and person.

The hardest discerning you will make in your career is often when to stay and when to leave, but I have seen too many people stay too long. And sometimes they stay for the wrong reasons. It could be fear, a false sense of loyalty, or just because they think they have no other option. It injures them, the rest of the team, and interrupts the progress toward a vision that hopefully is bigger than any one person.

Compromise

You can learn to live with what you have got in a leader. There are seasons in which you have no choice. You cannot find anything new and you need the work. (Sometimes we call those seasons "life.") There are also times God has placed you where you are for a reason.

Keep in mind, you will learn a lot from any situation, even under a controlling leader. If nothing more, you can use the time to reinforce how you will someday lead differently.

If you compromise—if you stay—you should remain loyal to the team and its values and mission. You should do your best work, have a positive attitude toward others, and attempt to make life better for those around you. Be obedient to God and respectful of authority, unless you are called to do something against your moral or personal values. This is the right thing to do. We do not get an excuse from biblical principles because we do not agree with the leadership. If you cannot, one of the other options should be your choice.

Collaborate

This is almost always the best option. Most leaders—even controlling leaders—have areas in which they are willing to admit they need help. Much of their willingness to do so will be based on the degree of trust placed in others or how important an issue is to them personally. Working to build a relationship of trust and seeking common ground on issues allow some people to excel under a controlling leader. If the leader sees you not as a threat but as a complement to their leadership, they may be more willing to invite your input. (You may need to go back to chapter 3 and reread the section about leading people who are supposed to be leading you.)

Getting to collaboration will require a risk on your part. You will have to gracefully challenge the controlling leadership. Like it or not, most complex issues do not disappear on their own. Two good questions to ask yourself are, Will I be content if this environment continues for the next year or longer? Do I think it is time to move on to something else? If the answer to both questions is no, then the best option may be to challenge the controlling leadership, attempting to get to some collaborative work, where you can do meaningful work for which you feel valued—and less controlled.

Note that you should not challenge anyone daily, so a challenge like this should be planned, considerate, and infrequent. But it may be the best option or the only one with which you can live. In some cases, you may need to do this in writing, so you can carefully craft what you want to say. It may take one person to introduce change for the rest of the organization.

Knowing how hard confronting a controlling leader can be, let me give you some suggestions as to how to challenge them.

Discern the need.

Pray about it. Talk it through with a few people you can trust with their confidence, emphasis on *few*. You should make sure your perception of this leader is correct. Is it them or is it you? Then ask yourself, Is this my responsibility? Do I sense the burden to do this? Will it make a difference? And if not, do I feel compelled to do it anyway?

Consider the timing.

When addressing any conflict, timing is everything. Pick a day when things appear to be going well from the leader's perspective. Find the least stressful, calmest time you can. You want to catch the leader in the best mood possible. If necessary, schedule an appointment with the leader.

Plan your approach.

What are you going to say? How will you say it? Will you do this alone or with someone else? You may want to write your response first and rehearse it. In stressful situations, I think it is okay to bring notes. It shows you came prepared and have thought about the issue. Make sure you show as much respect for the leader as you can. Balance your critique with ample genuine compliments. (There are even times, depending on the expected response of the leader or your expected ability to keep your composure, when I would recommend writing a letter.)

Bite the bullet.

You can keep putting it off, but at some point you will have to approach the controlling leader if you hope to see a change. It will never be easy, but who knows if you were not put in this place "for such a time as this" (Est. 4:14). And by this step you have already discerned the need to do this.

Couch your talk in love and respect.

This cannot be overemphasized. People do not listen to others who do not show genuine love for them or at least respect the things or people they love. Most controlling leaders are hungry for respect. It may even be part of their problem and why they control. So if you want to gain their attention, be respectful. (Again, because I know this is difficult for some people, being respectful does not mean being silent, just as being meek or gentle does not mean being weak.)

Momma always said, "You'll catch more flies with honey than with vinegar." The Bible says it another way: "A soft answer turns away wrath, / But a harsh word stirs up anger" (Prov. 15:1).

Be clear and direct.

Know that what you offer to the leader can add value to the team as well as the leader. Have some specific areas where you can collaborate with the leader. This is very important. Vagueness accomplishes nothing. Do not make the leader wonder what you are talking about when you confront them. Talking around the problem will not be clear to a controlling leader. Most controlling leaders think their control is a sign of good leadership. They do not realize they are the problem. You will not want to take this step to confront more than once, so make sure you are clear with the issues as you see them and how you want to help. If you are going through stress and preparation in order to confront, make sure you address the real problem.

Live with your consequences.

You have prayed and prepared. This is not something you will do very often. But if you know you are doing the right thing—you confronted the leader with love and respect, you were clear about the problem—then the response of the leader is out of your hands. You cannot control the leader's response, but you can control your response to the leader's response. Be willing to live with the consequences of your actions. This may be the one thing you end up modeling for the controlling leader.

CLOSING THOUGHTS

I want to close with one thing more that helps me not to be a controlling leader. I saved it for the end because I think it may be one of the most important things I can say to leaders. In fact, as I have spoken at conferences the last few years, I have tried to make it appropriate to close with this last bit of advice. It is one I have come to after years of experience.

I practice my Sabbath day and try to keep it holy.

I am sorry if this sounds too preachy for a leadership book, but I have learned that God knows best when it comes to following this command. I observe my Sabbath on Saturday most weeks. It is my day with Cheryl. It is not necessarily a day where I do nothing. I do not rest well by lying on the couch. It is a day where I do what I want to do. On my Sabbath, I do not work. I play. I rest. I recharge. I clear my head and prepare for the week ahead. I have learned I must be very self-aware of my limitations, my tendency to control, and my need for rest.

And on my Sabbath, I let everything I am supposed to be leading take care of itself for this day. How does this sound for a controlling leader?

I am asked frequently how I manage to keep a day set aside for me while leading a large organization.

First, I recognize the value of rest. I realize there is a reason to observe a Sabbath. If we value something enough, we will make it a priority. As important as any day is, my Sabbath is a must-do part of every week.

I place it on the calendar. And this is huge: I trust others to handle their responsibilities. Regardless of staff size, pastors need to surround themselves with some healthy people and take a risk on them. To do otherwise is to be controlling.

Truly observing the Sabbath will require empowerment. I also prepare for it. I handle any details I can in advance, but then I discipline myself to do it. I make myself take a day off.

Frankly, some will never understand the value of your Sabbath (even if they see the value for themselves), but they will also be the first to complain if you are not performing at your best in other areas of your ministry.

Please understand, there are no perfect plans. This works most of the time for me, but not all of the time. There are, of course, exceptions, interruptions, and kingdom opportunities that cause me to not protect every Sabbath day. I often get pushback from those who point out that Jesus consistently allowed interruptions. And I agree. But I have two counterpoints. First, Jesus only had three years of ministry, so he had to make the best use of his limited time. Second, and more important, we certainly see the value Jesus placed in intentionally getting away to rest.

As much as possible, however, I stick with this plan. And when it is interrupted, especially if it happens several weeks in a row, I will make up the time with some extra time away from my responsibilities. I try to get my downtime back at some point. It has become this important to me now.

Here is the crazy thing—and the God thing. When I practice this in my life, I am less controlling throughout the week. I have an easier time letting go of any attempt to control outcomes. And even better, many times, when I am most still, God does his greatest work in my life and where I am trying to lead. The best you can always do is place things in the hands of your Creator: "Now to Him who is able to do exceedingly abundantly above all that we ask or think, according to the power that works in us" (Eph. 3:20).

I have numerous examples of this verse and principle being proved true in my life, but one sticks out in my memory.

Within the slums of Brazil is a radio frequency assigned to one particular slum. Years ago, we were doing evangelism in one of the slums when I found out about this early in the week of our visit. Since I had a radio ministry at the time, we asked our host pastor if it were possible for me to be on the radio. They said no, because they had no connection to the slum's radio station. Usually the drug lords, because it is their means of disseminating information to the people, control the radio station. We accepted the fact that this was not something we would be able to do.

It would help you to understand the awesomeness of this story if you knew how these slums are laid out. They are difficult to navigate even if you live there. Some houses have numbers, most do not. When they have numbers, they are not in sequence but rather random. Houses are stacked on top of each other. It's quite confusing.

One afternoon, while trying to find a particular home we were supposed to visit, we stopped at a house to ask for directions. The home had a big dog, and from all appearances, it did not like us very much. We gladly stayed outside and talked to the lady of the house. As we were asking directions and getting to know her, we heard rapid gunfire. What had been a busy street quickly became deserted. We scrambled into the house, dog or no dog, and hit the floor.

You want to hear a God thing?

As we were lying on the floor, hiding from the gunshots, we struck up a conversation with the owner of the house. I asked if she had a job. Many do not, but some do. Yes, she told us. She ran the radio station for the village. She had recently become a Christian through another missionary group, but she didn't have a church home. She wanted me to join her on the radio. The church did not know where she was, but God did!

I introduced our new friend to the church pastor, and he promised to be a regular guest on the radio. God can do more than we can ever imagine!

Is there something you believe is impossible? Is there anything you have been trusting God with for so long, you are beginning to think it is no longer an option? Maybe you will get to the end of this book on leadership and feel overwhelmed with the ways you want or feel you need to improve. Continue praying and trusting God. God can do things beyond our wildest imagination.

If he can help us stumble across a hidden radio station in the middle of a densely populated, dangerous slum in Brazil, when even the people who live there couldn't find it, God can surely come through for you. And he will. Keep trusting!

Rest your soul, leader. Empower others and rest your soul. It is the best way to survive and thrive long term as a leader.

 **NOTES**

Introduction

1. John Maxwell, *The 21 Irrefutable Laws of Leadership* (Nashville, TN: Thomas Nelson, 2007), 16.

Myth 1: A Position Will Make Me a Leader

1. Michael Useem, *The Leadership Moment: Nine True Stories of Triumph and Disaster and Their Lessons for Us All*

Myth 2: If I Am Not Hearing Anyone Complain, Everyone Must be Happy

1. Jack Welch, *Winning* (New York: HarperCollins, 2005), 74.
2. Ron Edmondson, "Zig Ziglar: A Tribute and Interview," *RE Ron Edmondson* (29 November 2012), http://www.ronedmondson.com/2012/11/zig-ziglar-a-tribute-and-interview.html.
3. Bill Hybels, "2014 Global Leadership Summit, Session 1," *Live Intentionally* (14 August 2014), http://www.liveintentionally.org/2014/08/14/2014-global-leadership-summit-session-1-bill-hybels-gls14/.

Myth 3: I Can Lead Everyone the Same Way

1. For more information visit http://www.myersbriggs.org/my -mbti-personality-type/mbti-basics/.
2. For more information visit https://www.gallupstrengthscenter .com/?utm_source=homepage&utm_medium=webad&utm _campaign=strengthsdashboard.
3. For more information visit https://www.discprofile.com/.
4. Erin Meyer, *The Culture Map: Breaking Through the Invisible Boundaries of Global Business* (New York: Perseus Books Group, 2014), 13.

Myth 4: Leadership and Management Are the Same Thing

1. Robert J. Banks and Bernice M. Ledbetter, *Reviewing Leadership: A Christian Evaluation of Current Approaches* (Grand Rapids, MI: Baker, 2004), 17.
2. Raymond P. Rood, "How Then Should Organizations Live? Exploring a Process of International Collaborative Organization Development," *Genysys Group* (1997, revised 2006), http://textlab.io/doc/993755/how-then-should -organizations-live%3F. http://www.thegenysysgroup.com/.
3. Ibid.
4. Ibid.
5. Tracy Parks, "What is a Bottleneck?" *Simplicated* (17 July 2013), http://www.simplicated.com/component/k2/item/168-process -snags-what-is-a-bottleneck.

Myth 5: Being the Leader Makes Me Popular

1. I changed names for these illustrations, but the illustrations are true.
2. Bill Hybels, (3 August 2016), https://twitter.com/BillHybels.
3. Rachel Thompson, "Stakeholder Analysis," *Mind Tools* (2016), https://www.mindtools.com/pages/article/newPPM_07.htm.

Myth 6: Leaders Must Have Charisma and Be Extroverts

1. Isabel Briggs Myers, "MBTI Basics," *Myers & Briggs Foundation* (2016), http://www.myersbriggs.org/my-mbti-personality-type /mbti-basics/.
2. Ibid.

Myth 7: Leaders Accomplish by Controlling Others

1. Gallup, Inc. "Command," *Strengths Transform* (10 February 2016), http://www.strengthstransform.com/strengths -descriptions/strengthsfinder-singapore-command/. Copyright © 2000, 2012 Gallup, Inc. All rights reserved. Gallup®, StrengthsFinder®, and each of the 34 StrengthsFinder theme names are trademarks of Gallup, Inc.
2. Gallup, Inc. "Command," https://www.hillcollege.edu/faculty _staff/StrengthsQuest/SQ_files/ITS%20POWER%20AND%20 EDGE/Command.pdf. Copyright © 2000, 2012 Gallup, Inc. All rights reserved. Gallup®, StrengthsFinder®, and each of the 34 StrengthsFinder theme names are trademarks of Gallup, Inc.

ABOUT THE AUTHOR

CREDIT: HEATHER KENNEDY BROWN

RON EDMONDSON IS A PASTOR WITH a heart for the established church and church planting. With a long business background, he brings a fresh approach to Christian leadership. Ron is pastor of the historic Immanuel Baptist Church in Lexington, Kentucky. He blogs regularly at RonEdmondson.com. Ron and his wife, Cheryl, live as empty-nesters with their spoiled Yorkiepoo named Lexi.

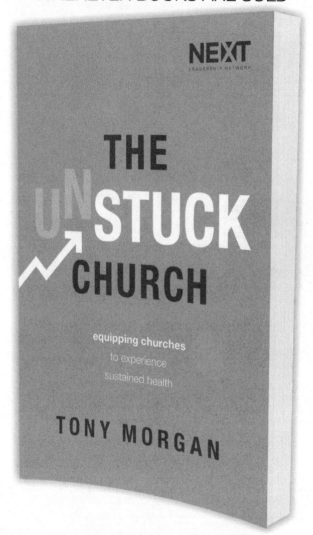